BUT HOW DO IT KNOW?

The Basic Principles of Computers
For Everyone

By

J. Clark Scott

Published by John C. Scott, Oldsmar, FL 34677

ISBN 978-0-615-30376-5

buthowdoitknow.com

Cover art, photography and design by Alexander C. Scott III
artbyalexscott.com

Printed in the United States of America

First Edition : July 2009

10 9 8 7 6 5 4 3 2 1

Table of Contents

iv

Introduction

The title of this book is the punch line of an old joke that goes like this:

Joe is a very nice fellow, but has always been a little slow. He goes into a store where a salesman is standing on a soapbox in front of a group of people. The salesman is pitching the miracle new invention, the Thermos bottle. He is saying, "It keeps hot food hot, and cold food cold...." Joe thinks about this a minute, amazed by this new invention that is able to make a decision about which of two different things it is supposed to do depending on what kind of food you put in it. He can't contain his curiosity, he is jumping up and down, waving his arm in the air, saying "but, but, but, but..." Finally he blurts out his burning question "But how do it know?"

You may or may not have laughed at the joke, but the point is that Joe looked at what this Thermos bottle could do, and decided that it must be capable of sensing something about its contents, and then performing a heating or cooling operation accordingly. He thought it must contain a heater and a refrigerator. He had no idea of the much simpler principle on which it actually operates, which is that heat always attempts to move from a hotter area to a cooler area, and all the Thermos does is to slow down this movement. With cold contents, the outside heat is slowed on its way in, and with hot contents, the heat is slowed on its way out. The bottle doesn't have to "know" in order to fulfill its mission, and doesn't heat or cool anything. And eventually, the contents, hot or cold, do end up at room temperature. But Joe's concept of how the bottle worked was far more complicated than the truth.

So the reason for the book title, is that when it comes to computers, people look at them, see what they can do, and imagine all sorts of things that must be in these machines. Or they imagine all sorts of principles that they must be based on, and therefore what they may be capable of. People may assign human qualities to the machine. And more than a few find themselves in situations where they feel that they are embarrassing themselves, like our friend in the joke, Joe.

But computers are actually quite easy to understand. Of course computers have a greater number of parts than a Thermos bottle, but each part is extremely simple, and they all operate on a very simple, very easy to understand principle.

With the Thermos, the principle is that of the motion of heat. This is something we can observe in life. We see ice cubes melting when they are removed from the freezer, and we see the hot meal cooling off on the table when the family is late for dinner.

In the computer, the principle on which it operates has to do with electricity, but that doesn't mean that it is hard to understand. If you have observed the fact that when you turn on a light switch, a light bulb lights up, and when you turn the switch off, the light goes dark, then you have observed the principle on which computers operate. That is about all you need to know about electricity to understand computers.

Just the Facts Ma'am

This book is not primarily intended to be a textbook. There are no problems to do at the end of each chapter. Its intention is simply to demystify the subject of computers for anyone who has ever wondered what's going on inside of that box. Of course, it also makes a perfect introduction to computers for a young person who will ultimately go on to get a PhD in Computer Science. But it should be easily understandable by housewives, senior citizens and children who can read well. It should be understandable to plumbers and street sweepers. It requires no previous technical education. It only requires that you can read the language, you can turn a light bulb on and off, and you can do very simple addition on the order of 8+5=13.

This book presents the complete essentials that make up a computer. It presents every piece and part, in the proper order so that each one will make sense, and can be understood. Every part is explained fully, and every new word is defined thoroughly when it is first used. Any attempt to simplify the subject further would leave gaps in the big picture where someone would still have to guess how the parts work together, and you just wouldn't ever have that "Aha, I get it!" moment that I think you'll soon have.

This book is not a 'dumbed-down' version of some college textbook. It is a complete explanation of the basic principles of computers. It is a technical book, but so is a cookbook and so is a driver's education handbook. This book just starts at the beginning and defines every item needed to understand the machine. No matter what someone already knows about computers, this will fill in any missing pieces and put them all together into something that makes sense.

Even our friend, Joe, could understand this book with diligent study. There are thousands of words and ideas associated with the field of computers that make the whole subject seem like a mess. But the basic concepts underlying them are simple.

In this book, there will not be volumes of trivia about the construction or history of computers, just the essentials, no more and no less. Each part of the computer has a simple function, and when they are connected together, you end up with a useful machine called a computer.

There is nothing to memorize in this book. Each chapter is designed to give you a new idea that you didn't have before, or if it is something that you had heard about previously, it always seemed confusing. Each idea is very simple, and one thing leads to the next. Each chapter presents an idea. Each idea is simple and easy to understand. Later chapters present ideas that build on the ideas from previous chapters.

If someone were to write a book about how to build a house, there could be various levels of detail. The simplest book would say, "lay a foundation, put up the walls, cover with a roof, put in plumbing and electrical, and you're done." That would not be enough detail for someone who didn't already have some experience using a hammer and saw and installing a faucet and wiring a light switch.

At the other end of the spectrum would be a book that had separate chapters for every possible type of foundation, the different kinds of dirt you might have to dig in, formulas for a dozen different kinds concrete, charts of weather conditions that are optimum for laying foundations, etc. That would be far too much information. There would be so many details, that what was really important would get lost.

This book attempts to give just enough detail to see what every computer has in common and how they work, not how to build the biggest or best computer ever made. It is not about any specific brand of computer. It is not about how to use a computer. If it were a book about building a house, it would probably describe a simple plan for a sturdy garden shed with a sink and one bare light bulb, showing the size and shape of every piece of wood, where to put all the nails, how to hang the door and how to put the water pipes together so they wouldn't leak. It would not show how to build anything as complicated as a fancy curved oak staircase.

We are going to show the one simple part that computers are made of, and then connect a bunch of them together until we have built a complete computer. It is going to be a lot simpler than you ever imagined.

Speed

Computers seem mysterious and magical. How can they do what they do? They play games, they draw pictures, they 'know' your credit rating. These machines are capable of doing all sorts of strange and wondrous things. Yet they *are* simple. They can do only a very few, very simple things. And, they can only do one of these simple things at a time. They appear to be doing complex things, only because they do a huge number of simple things one after another in a small amount of time. The result, as in a video game, is very complex in appearance, but in reality, is very simple, just very very fast.

Computers are designed to do a small number of specific simple things, and to do these things quickly, one after the other. Which simple things are done, and in what order, determines what sort of task the computer accomplishes in any given time, but anything the computer does consists of nothing outside of its limited capabilities.

Once you see what a computer is made up of, you will come to realize how it is that they can do what they do, exactly what sorts of things they are capable of, and also, what they are not capable of.

So the secret of computers is not that they are complex, rather it is their speed. Let's look at exactly how fast their speed is.

Since computers work on electricity, their speed is related to the speed of electricity. You may remember hearing that the speed of light is 186,000 miles per second. That's pretty darned fast. Light can go around the entire earth seven times in one second, or from the Earth to the Moon in about a second and a half. Per the physicists, electricity has many properties in common with light, and its speed, when traveling in a wire, gets slowed down to about half the speed of light. But still, going all the way around the Earth three and a half times in one second is extremely fast.

As a point of comparison, imagine it is a hot day and you have an electric fan sitting on the table blowing cool air on you. The fan is spinning around so fast that the blades are a blur, but it is only spinning around about 40 times each second. A point on the edge of one of those blades will only travel about 150 feet in that second, it will take 35 seconds for that point to travel just one mile.

Since the fan blades are already a blur, it may be hard to imagine them going just ten times faster. If it did, that fan would be putting out quite a breeze. And if you could make it go a hundred times faster, it would almost certainly self-destruct, with fan blades breaking off and getting stuck in the ceiling. But electricity traveling in the same circle would go around about a hundred million times in one second, that's two and a half million times faster than the fan blades. That's fast.

A million is a very large number. If you took a big sheet of paper that was 40 inches square and took a ruler and placed it at the top edge, and drew 25 dots per inch along the top edge of the paper, you would have to draw one thousand dots to get across that sheet of paper. If you then moved the ruler down the page 1/25th of an inch, and drew another thousand dots, and kept doing that, you would have to move the ruler down the page one thousand times, each time drawing one thousand dots. If you could complete such a boring task, you would end up with a piece of paper with a million dots on it. That's a lot of dots or a lot of anything. And just to finish the thought, if you could find a thousand people who would each draw one of these million dot sheets, and stacked up those thousand sheets in a pile, you would then have a billion dots.

Now let's say that the electricity moving around inside the computer can accomplish some simple task by traveling one foot. That means that the computer could do 500 million simple things in one second. Again for comparison, the fan on the table will spin for 7 hours to go around just one million times and it will take a full six months for it to spin around 500 million times.

When you talk about the speed that electricity can move between parts inside the computer, some of the parts you can see are a foot apart, some are closer, an inch, a tenth of an inch. And inside these parts are a multitude more parts that are very close to each other, some just thousandths of an inch apart. And the shorter the distance the electricity has to travel, the sooner it gets there.

There is no point in saying how many things today's computers do in a single second, because that would date this book. Computer manufacturers continue to produce new computers that go twice as fast as the fastest computers of only two or three years past. There is a theoretical limit to how fast they can go, but engineers keep finding practical ways to get around the theories and make machines that go faster and faster.

During all of this time that computers have been getting faster, smaller and cheaper, the things that computers do, really have not changed since they were first invented in the 1940's. They still do the same few simple things, just faster, cheaper, more reliably and in a smaller package.

There are only a few sections to a computer, and they are all made out of the same kinds of parts. Each section has a specific mission, and the combination of these parts into a machine was a truly marvelous invention. But it is not difficult to understand.

Language

In this book, we are going to need to define some words that are used to describe the parts inside a computer.

In some professions, notably the Medical and Legal, there is a tendency to make up a lot of new words, and to take them from the ancient Greek and Latin languages, and to make them long and hard to pronounce.

In the world of computers, it seems that the pioneer inventors were a less formal sort of people. Most of the words they used are simple words from everyday language, words that already existed, but are used in a new way.

Some of the new words are words we already know, used as a different part of speech, like an existing noun now used as a verb. Some of the words are acronyms, the first letters from the words of a phrase.

Each word will be described thoroughly when it is first used. And although there are thousands of words and acronyms in use if you consider the entire computer industry, there are only about a dozen or two words needed to understand the computer itself. You have probably heard some of these words before, and figured out what they meant from how they were used, but now you will get the proper and full definitions. In many cases you may find that they are simpler than you thought.

Just a Little Bit

What is in a computer? It shows you still pictures, moving pictures, music, your checkbook, letters you have written, it plays video games, communicates all around the world, and much much more. But are there pictures inside the computer? If you got out a microscope and knew where to look, could you find little pictures somewhere inside the computer? Would you see "A"s and "B"s and "8"s and "12"s moving around in there somewhere?

The answer is no, there are no pictures, numbers or letters in a computer. There is only one kind of thing in a computer. There are a large number of this kind of thing, but there is only one kind of thing in there. It is called a bit.

When you flip a coin up in the air, and let it fall on the ground, it will end up on the floor in one of two possible states - with either the head showing, or the tail.

The light in your living room (assuming you have a switch and not a dimmer) can be either on or off.

The lock on your front door can be either locked or unlocked.

What do all of these things have in common? They are all places that contain a thing that can be in one of two possible states. This is the definition of a bit.

A bit is some kind of a physical object that has a size and a location in space, and it has some quality about itself, that at any given time can be in one of two possible states, and may be made to change back and forth between those two states.

A lump of clay is not a bit. It can be molded into a ball, a cube, a pancake, a ring, a log, a face or anything else you can think of. It has a size and a location in space, but there are too many states that it can be in for it to be called a bit. If you took that lump of clay, flattened it out, scratched "yes" on one side of it, and "no" on the other side, and then put it in a kiln and fired it until it was hard, then you might be able to call it a bit. It could sit on a table with either the "yes" or "no" showing. Then it would only have two states.

You have probably heard of bits before in relation to computers, and now you know what they are. In a computer, the bits are not like the coin or the lock, they are most like the light. That is, the bits in a computer are places that either have electricity or they do not. In a computer, the bits are very, very small and there are a very large number of bits, but that's all that is in there.

Like the light in the living room, the bit is either on or off. In the living room, there is electricity in the wall coming into the switch. When you turn the switch on, the electricity goes from the switch, through the wires in the wall and ceiling, into the light socket and then into the light bulb. So this bit in the living room is several feet long, it includes the switch, the wires, the socket and the light bulb. In a computer, bits are mostly tiny, actually microscopic. Also, the computer bit doesn't have a mechanical switch at one end or a light bulb at the other. If you removed the light bulb from the socket in the living room, the switch would still send electricity to the socket when it was on, and it would still be a bit – you just wouldn't be able to see whether it was on or off by looking at a light bulb. Your computer has something resembling switches, like the keys on the keyboard, and something resembling light bulbs, like the tiny dots on the screen, but most of the bits are inside and unseen.

This is basically all there is in a computer – bits. There are lots and lots of them, and they are arranged and connected up in various ways, which we will examine in detail as the book progresses, but this is what is inside all computers – bits. A bit is always in one of its two possible states, either off or on, and they change between on and off when they are told to do so. Computer bits aren't like the coin that has to physically flip over to change from one state to the other. Bits don't change shape or location, they don't look any different, they don't move or rotate or get bigger or smaller. A computer bit is just a place, if there is no electricity in that place, then the bit is off. When electricity is present, then the bit is on.

If you want to change a coin from showing heads to showing tails, you have to physically move it to flip it over, which takes some amount of time. Because the only thing that has to move in a computer bit is the electricity, changing it's state from off to on, or on to off can happen much more quickly than anything that has to be moved physically.

As another example, remember the wild American west from the movies? There were little towns separated by vast distances. The bigger towns would have a telegraph office. In this office was a guy wearing a funny hat who had a spring-loaded switch called a key, and he would send messages by pressing this key on and off in certain patterns that represented the letters of the alphabet. That key was connected to a battery (yes they had batteries back then) and a wire that was strung along poles until it got to another town. The key simply connected the battery to the wire when it was pressed, and disconnected the battery when the key was not pressed. In the other town there was another telegraph office, the wire came into that office, the end of it was wrapped around an iron rod (which turns into a magnet when there is electricity in the wire,) the magnetized rod attracted a little bar of iron held nearby with a spring, and made a clicking sound every time the electricity came on. The guy in the office listened to the pattern of the clicking and wrote down the letters of the message. They might have used a light bulb instead of the clicker, except that light bulbs had not yet been invented.

The point of bringing up this subject, is that this whole telegraph machine, from the key that gets pressed in one town, through the long wire that travels to another town many miles away, to the clicker, this whole apparatus comprises just one single bit. It is a place that can either have or not have electricity, and goes on and off as it is told. And this method of communication revolutionized the world in many ways. But this very important invention of the 1840s consisted of nothing more than one bit.

So I hope this begins to simplify the subject of computers for you. There is only one thing inside computers, bits. Lots of them to be sure, but when you understand bits, you understand what's in there.

What the...?

Imagine it is a bright sunny day, and you walk into a room with lots of open windows. You notice that the ceiling light is on. You decide that this is a waste, and you are going to turn the light off. You look at the wall next to the door and see a switch plate with two switches. So you assume that the one closer to the door is for the ceiling light. But then you notice that the switch is already off. And the other switch is off too. So then you think "well, maybe someone installed the switch upside down," so you decide to flip the switch anyway. You flip it on and off but nothing happens, the ceiling light stays lit. So then you decide that it must be the other switch, and you flip it on, off, on, off. Again nothing happens, that ceiling light continues to shine at you. You look around, there is no other door, there are no other switches, no apparent way to turn off this darned light. It just has to be one of these two switches, who built this crazy house anyway? So you grab one switch with each hand and start flipping them wildly. Then suddenly you notice the ceiling light flicker off briefly. So you slow down your switch flipping and stop when the ceiling light is off. Both switches say "on", and the light is now off. You turn one switch off, then on, and the light goes on, then back off. This is backwards. One switch off equals light on? So then you turn the other switch off, then on, the same thing, the light goes on, then back off. What the heck? Anyway, you finally figure out how it works. If both switches are on, the light goes off. If one or the other or both switches are off, then the ceiling light is on. Kind of goofy, but you accomplish what you intended, you turn both switches on, the light goes off, and you get the heck out of this crazy room.

Now what is the purpose of this little story about the odd light switches? The answer is, that in this chapter we are going to present the most basic part that computers are made of. This part works exactly like the lighting system in that strange room.

This computer part is a simple device that has three connections where there may or may not be some electricity. Two of those connections are places where electricity may be put into the device, and the third connection is a place where electricity may come out of the device.

Of the three connections, two of them are called "inputs," because electricity can be sent to them from somewhere else. The third connection is called the "output" because electricity can come out of it and then be sent somewhere else.

This computer part is a device that does something with bits. If you have two bits, and you connect those two bits to the inputs, this device "looks" at those two bits, and "decides" whether to turn the one output bit on or off.

The way it "decides" is very simple, and is always the same. If both inputs are on, the output will be off. If one or both of the inputs are off, then the output will be on. That's just the way that the room with the odd light switches worked.

Remember that there is nothing but bits inside the computer. This simple device is where bits come from and where they go to. The "decision" that this device makes is how bits come to be turned on and off in a computer.

Two bits go into the device, and one bit comes out. Two bits come from somewhere else, are examined by the device, and a new third bit is generated so that it may go somewhere else.

If you have been extra observant, you may have asked yourself this question: "when both inputs are off, the output is on, so.... how do you get electricity at the output if both inputs are off?" Well, that is an excellent question, and the excellent answer is that every one of these devices is also connected to power. Like every appliance or table lamp in your house, where each has a plug with two pins, this device has a pair of wires, one of which is connected to a place where the electricity is always on, and the other is connected to a place where the electricity is always off. This is where the electricity for the output comes from. When someone builds a computer, they have to make all of those power connections to each one of those parts in order to have it work, but when we are drawing diagrams of parts, how they are connected, and what they will do, we won't bother drawing the power wires – they would just clutter up the drawing. It is understood that each part has its power connection, and we don't worry about it. Just understand that it is there, and we won't mention it any more for the rest of the book. I wouldn't have even mentioned it here except that I figured that you'd probably ask yourself that question sooner or later.

Now I know I said that you don't have to understand much about electricity to understand computers. Here is as complicated as it gets. There are actually a half dozen electronic parts inside of this device that make it work, but we are not going to examine those parts in this book. Someone who has an electronics background could look at what's in there, and in about 30 seconds would say "Oh yeah, if both inputs are on, the output will be off, and for any other combination the output will be on, just like the book says." And then that person could go ahead and read this book without ever having to think about what's in there again. Someone who doesn't know electronics misses out on those few seconds of understanding, but this book is the same for everyone.

In normal house wiring, one switch turns one light on and off. In the computer, it takes two switches, and it's sort of backwards in that they both have to be on to turn the light off. But if you accept the fact that something could be made that operates this way, you can then understand how everything in the computer works.

This type of computer part is in fact the ONLY type of part required to build a computer. Of course it takes a lot of them to build a complete computer, but with enough of them, you can make any type of computer. So there you go again, see how simple a computer is? It is just full of this little type of thing – a lot of them to be sure, but this is all there is.

Now we need to give this device a name, this thing inside the computer that bits are made of, it is called a "gate." I can't find a good reason why it is called a gate, a gate in a fence lets people through when it is open, and stops people when it is closed. A computer gate generates a third bit from two other bits, it doesn't open and close or stop or let anything through. The meaning of this computer term "gate" doesn't seem to fit into the common meaning of the word, but sorry, I didn't make up the name, that's just what it is called. You'll get used to it. At least it isn't some long word from the ancient Greek.

In the next few chapters, we are going to show how we can do something useful by connecting several gates together. We will use drawings like the following. The 'D' shape with the little circle at its tip represents the device we have described, and the lines represent the wires going in and coming out of it that get attached to other parts of the computer. The picture on the left shows a gate complete with its power wires, but as promised, we won't be concerned with them for the rest of this book. The drawing on the right shows everything we need:

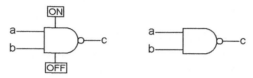

This is a representation of a gate. The two wires on the left (a and b) are the inputs, and the wire on the right (c) is the output. All three wires are bits, which means that they are either on or off. Each input bit comes from somewhere else in the computer and is either on or off depending on what is happening where it came from, and then this gate sets its output on or off depending on the states of its two inputs.

Sometimes it is useful to make a little chart that shows how the various input combinations create the output, like this:

a	b	c
Off	Off	On
Off	On	On
On	Off	On
On	On	Off

Each line shows one possible combination of the inputs, and what the output will be under those circumstances.

Compare this little chart with the experience with the odd room with the two light switches. If one switch is called 'a,' the other switch is called 'b,' and the ceiling light is called 'c,' then this little chart describes completely and exactly how the equipment in that room operates. The only way to get that light off is to have both switch 'a' and switch 'b' on.

Simple Variations

As mentioned, this gate is the only thing you need to build a computer, but you need a lot of them, and they have to be wired together in an intelligent manner in order to be able to make them do something useful. What we are going to do here is to show two simple things that are done many times inside any computer.

This first one is very simple. Take the gate above, and take the two input wires, 'a' and 'b,' and tie them together. Thus 'a' and 'b' will always be the same. They can still be changed on and off, but 'a' and 'b' can never be different. 'A' and 'b' can either both be on, or both be off. Thus the chart of this combination only has two lines on it, two possibilities:

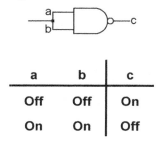

a	b	c
Off	Off	On
On	On	Off

Actually, since columns 'a' and 'b' are the same, there is really only one input and it can be drawn simply like this with a triangle instead of the 'D' shape. Its chart is also very simple:

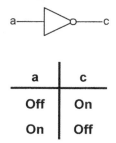

a	c
Off	On
On	Off

For our second variation, lets combine one of our original type of gate with the new gate that we just invented, like this:

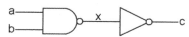

And we'll combine the charts of how they work. The 'a,' 'b' and 'x' are like the first gate, the 'x' and 'c' are like the second gate.

a	b	x	c
Off	Off	On	Off
Off	On	On	Off
On	Off	On	Off
On	On	Off	On

This combination is used so often inside computers, that it is built as a single unit, and the 'x' bit is not available to connect to. So to make it simpler to understand, it is drawn as a single unit like this:

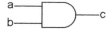

The only difference between this picture and the picture of our original gate is that the little circle after the big 'D' is missing.

Since 'x' is not used, the chart can also be simplified, and it looks like this:

a	b	c
Off	Off	Off
Off	On	Off
On	Off	Off
On	On	On

The only difference between this chart and the chart of our original gate is that every item in column 'c' is the opposite of what it was in the original chart.

Imagine that this combination of gates was installed in that room with the two light switches and the ceiling light. The only way the light could be on is if both switches were on. So if you walked in there and saw the light on, and then looked at the switches, you would see that they were both on. No matter which switch you decided was for the light, and you switched it off, the light would go off. You might not notice that if you turned both off, and then wanted to turn the light back on, you wouldn't be able to do it by just flipping one switch. You would have to go through the same experiment, flipping both switches until the light came on, and you would find that one switch <u>and</u> the other switch would have to be on to get the light to light.

This combination gate could be described this way: For the output to be on, one input AND the other input must both be on. Thus this type of gate has a name, and in the tradition of the informal terminology invented by computer people, because it reminds us of what the word AND means, it is simply called an "AND gate."

Now to fill in a few details purposely left out above, the original gate we looked at works like the AND gate except the output is the opposite, or the negative of the AND gate. Thus it is called a Negative AND gate, or just a "NAND gate" for short.

The simple gate that had both inputs tied together also has its own name. The output is always the opposite of the one input, that is, if the input is on, the output is not on (off.) If the input is off, the output is not off (on.) The output is always NOT what the input is, thus, it is called a "NOT gate."

Notice the difference between the diagrams of the AND gate and the NAND gate. They are the same except that there is a little circle at the beginning of the output of the NAND gate. The thing that looks like a large letter 'D' means to do the 'AND' function, which means to take action only if both inputs are on, and the little circle means switch to the opposite. So an AND gate is on if both inputs are on, a NAND gate is off if both inputs are on. The NOT gate starts with a triangle, which just means take the input and turn it into an output. The circle then means to switch to the opposite.

The AND gate is used a lot in computers, and it is probably the easiest to understand, but we looked at the NAND gate first for two reasons. The first and less important reason is that the NAND gate is the easiest gate to build. When you have to build a large number of gates, it will be cheaper and more reliable if you can use the type of gate that is easiest to build.

The second, and very important reason that we looked at the NAND gate first is this: That everything in a computer that makes it a computer, can be made out of one or more NAND gates. We have already seen that the NOT gate and the AND gate can be made out of NAND gates, and we will see a few more interesting combinations as we go along. But every one of them is based on this silly little thing called a NAND gate.

The problem in this chapter has been that the NAND gate is the basic building block of computers, but the AND gate is the first gate that has a name that makes sense. So we looked first at the NAND gate and the NOT gate without giving them names. Then we built an AND gate, gave it its name, and went back and named the first two.

As a note on the language here, the word 'and' is a conjunction in regular English. It connects two things, as in "I like peas and carrots." In computers, we use the word in two new ways. First, it is an adjective, a word that modifies a noun. When we say "this is an AND gate," the word "gate" is a noun, and the word "AND" tells us what kind of a gate it is. This is how "AND" has been used in this chapter. "AND" will also be used as a verb, as in "let us AND these two bits." We will see AND used in this way later in the book.

So back to the simplicity theme of this book, we have said that there is only one thing in computers, bits. And now we see that bits are constructed using gates, and all gates come down to the NAND gate. So all you have to know to understand computers is this very simple device, the NAND gate. No kidding! Can you understand this thing? Then you can understand the whole computer.

Diagrams

If you want to see how a mechanical machine works, the best way to do it is to look inside of it, watch the parts move as it operates, disassemble it, etc. The second best way is to study it from a book that has a lot of pictures showing the parts and how they interact.

A computer is also a machine, but the only thing that moves inside of it is the invisible and silent electricity. It is very boring to watch the inside of a computer, it doesn't look like anything is happening at all.

The actual construction of the individual parts of a computer is a very interesting subject, but we are not going to cover it any further than to say the following: The technique starts with a thin crystal wafer, and in a series of steps, it is subjected to various chemicals, photographic processes, heat and vaporized metal. The result is something called a 'chip,' which has millions of electronic parts constructed on its surface. The process includes connecting the parts into gates, and connecting the gates into complete computer sections. The chip is then encased in a piece of plastic that has pins coming out of it. Several of these are plugged into a board, and there you have a computer. The computer we are going to 'build' in this book could easily fit on one chip less than a quarter of an inch square.

But the point is, that unlike a mechanical machine, the actual structure of a chip is very cluttered and hard to follow, and you can't see the electricity anyway. The diagrams we saw in the previous chapter are the best way to show how a computer works, so we'd better get pretty good at reading them.

Throughout the rest of this book, we are going to build new parts by connecting several gates together. We will describe what the new part does, and then give it a name and its own symbol. Then we may connect several of those new parts into something else that also gets a name and a symbol. Before you know it, we will have assembled a complete computer.

Every time there is a new diagram, the text will explain what its purpose is, and how the parts achieve it, but the reader really must look the diagram over until it can be seen that the gates actually do what the book says they will do. If this is done faithfully with each one, you will very shortly see exactly how a computer works.

There are only two things in our drawings, there are parts that have inputs and outputs, and there are lines, or wires, that connect outputs and inputs together.

When electricity comes out of the output of a gate, the electricity travels through the whole wire as fast as it can go. If the output of a gate is on, then the electricity is on in the wire that is connected to it, for as far as it goes. If the output of a gate is off, the whole wire is off. I guess you could consider that the bit that comes out of the gate includes the whole wire as well.

The inputs of gates do not use up the electricity in the wire, so one output may be connected to the input of one or many gates.

When wires are connected together, this is shown by a dot where they meet on the diagram, and all wires that are connected together get electricity as if they were one wire. When wires cross on a diagram without a dot, it means that there is no connection between them, they are not touching, the two bits are separate.

Whenever there is a choice, the diagrams will show the path of the electricity moving from left to right, or from the top of the page towards the bottom. However, there will be many exceptions to this, especially later on in the book. But you can always tell which way the electricity is moving in a wire by starting at an output and following it to an input.

Most of the diagrams in the book are very easy to follow. In a few cases, there will also be one of those charts that shows what the output will be for every possible combination of inputs. If you have trouble following a diagram, you can pencil in the ons and offs right on the page, or place coins on the page and flip them so that heads means on and tails means off.

Unfortunately, the diagram in the next chapter is probably the hardest one to follow in the whole book, but once you master it, you'll be an expert diagram reader.

Remember When

You have probably heard of computer memory, and now we are going to see exactly what that is. Since the only thing inside of computers is bits, and the only thing that happens to bits is that they either turn on or turn off, then it follows that the only thing a computer can 'remember' is whether a bit was on or off. We will now see how that is accomplished.

The following diagram shows one bit of computer memory. It happens to be one of the neatest tricks you can do with a few gates. We will examine how it works here at great length, and after we understand it, we will replace it with its own symbol, and use it as a building block for bigger and better things.

It is made of only four NAND gates, but its wiring is kind of special. Here it is:

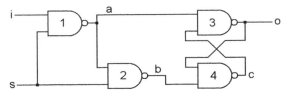

This combination as a whole has two inputs and one output. 'I' is where we input the bit that we want to remember, and 'o' is the output of the remembered bit. 'S' is an input that tells these gates when to 'set' the memory. There are also three internal wires labeled 'a', 'b' and 'c' that we will have to look at to see how these parts work together. Try to follow this carefully, once you see that it works, you will understand one of the most important and most commonly used things in a computer.

To see how this works, start with 's' on and 'i' off. Since 'i' and 's' go into gate 1, one input is off, so 'a' will be on. Since 'a' and 's' go to gate 2, both inputs are on, and therefore 'b' will be off. Looking at gate 4, since 'b' is off, the output of gate 4, 'c' will be on. Since 'c' and 'a' are both on, the output of gate 3, 'o' will be off. 'O' goes back down to gate 4 providing a second off input, leaving 'c' still on. The important thing to note here is that with 's' on, 'o' ends up the same as 'i.'

Now with 's' still on, lets change 'i' to on. Since 'i' and 's' go into gate 1, 'a' will be off. 'A' goes to one side of both gate 2 and gate 3, therefore their outputs 'o' and 'b' must both be on. 'O' and 'b' both on go into gate 4 and turn 'c' off, which goes back up to gate 3 providing it with a second off input, leaving 'o' still on. The important thing to note here is the same thing we noted in the previous paragraph - that with 's' on, 'o' ends up the same as 'i.'

So far, we have seen that when 's' is on, you can change 'i' on and off, and 'o' will change with it. 'O' will go on and off just the same as 'i.' With 's' on, this combination is no more useful than a wire connecting 'i' to 'o.'

Now let's see what happens when we turn 's' off. Look at gate 1. When 's' is off, 'a' will be on no matter what you do to 'i.' Now you can switch 'i' on and off and nothing will happen. The same goes for gate 2. 'A' may be on, but 's' is off, so 'b' can only be on. Both 'a' and 'b' are on, and changing 'i' does nothing. Now the only thing left that matters, the big question is, what will 'o' be?

If 'i' and 'o' were on before 's' got turned off, gate 3 had both inputs off, and gate 4 had both inputs on. When 's' goes off, 'a' comes on, which is one input to gate 3. But the other input is off, so nothing changes, 'o' stays on.

If 'i' and 'o' were off before 's' got turned off, gate 3 had both inputs on, and gate 4 had both inputs off. When 's' goes off, 'b' comes on, which is one input to gate 4. But the other input is off, so nothing changes, 'c' stays on and 'o' stays off.

So the answer to the question of what happens to 'o' when 's' is turned off, is that it stays the way it was, and it is no longer affected by 'i.'

Now what do we have here? With 's' on, 'o' does whatever 'i' does. With 's' off, 'o' stays the way it and 'i' were, at the last instant just before 's' went off. Now 'i' can change, but 'o' stays the way it was. This combination of gates locks in the way 'i' was at an earlier time. This is how a combination of four NAND gates can "remember." This is only one bit of memory, but this is the basic building block of all computer memory. All that computer memory is, is a way of preserving the way a bit was set at some point in time.

I hope you followed the wires and the ons and offs in this chapter. Once you see exactly how this thing works, you will know that these simple NAND gates can create a memory bit, and I assure you that you will never wonder about it again.

Now that we know how this thing works, we no longer need to look at that tricky internal wiring of this combination. We have seen how it works, and from now on, we will just use this diagram to represent it:

'I' is the input bit that you want to save. 'S' is the input that allows 'i' into the memory bit when 's' is on, and locks it in place or 'sets' it when 's' goes off. 'O' is the output of the current or saved data. 'M' stands for Memory. Pretty simple, eh?

Let's go back to our room with the funny light switches. It had a NAND gate hooked up in it. Let's take the NAND gate out and replace it with this new memory bit. We'll connect the left switch to the 'i' wire, the right switch to the 's' wire, and the ceiling light to the 'o' wire. We could start out with everything looking the same, that is, the light is on, but both switches are off. That would mean that at some point in the past, both 'i' and 's' were on, and 's' got turned off first, locking the then state of 'i' into our memory bit, which then comes out at 'o.' Then 'i' could have been switched off without affecting anything. So if we walked in and decided that we wanted to turn the light off, we would first try the 'i' switch, turn it on and off, and nothing would happen. Then we would try the 's' switch. When we turn it on, the light would go off. Aha we say, the 's' switch controls the light, but it is installed up-side-down! So then we turn the 's' switch back off, expecting the light to come back on, but the light remains off. Now the switches are in the same position as they were when we entered the room, they're both off, but now the light is off as well, boy is this confusing. Now I don't want to speculate on how much cursing would go on before someone figured this out, but in the end they would find that when 's' was on, the light went on and off with 'i,' and when 's' was off, the light would stay the way it was just before 's' got turned off.

What Can We Do With A Bit?

Now we have described a bit, we have shown how to build one, how to remember over time what state a bit was in at an earlier instant in time, now what? What do we do with it?

Since a bit is actually nothing more than the electricity being on or off, the only actual, real thing we can do with a bit is to turn lights on or off, or toasters or whatever.

But we can also use a bit to represent something else in our lives. We can take a bit, and connect it to a red light, and say that when this bit is on, it means stop, and when this bit is off, you may go. Or if a particular bit is on, you want fries with your burger; if it is off, you want the burger only.

This is the action of using a code. What is a code? A code is something that tells you what something else means. When something is supposed to mean something, somewhere someone has to make a list of all of the states of the 'thing,' and the meanings associated with each of those states. When it comes to a bit, since it only can be in two different states, then a bit can only mean one of two things. A code for a bit would only need two meanings, and one of those meanings would be associated with the bit being off, and the other meaning would be associated with the bit being on.

This is how you assign meaning to a bit. The bit does not contain any meaning in and of itself; there is no room in a bit for anything other than the presence or absence of electricity. Meaning is assigned to a bit by something external to the bit. There is nothing about traffic or French fries in a bit, we are just saying that for this bit in this place, connected to a red light hanging over an intersection, when it is on, you must stop, when it is off, you may go. Another bit, in a cash register in a fast food restaurant, means put fries in the bag when the bit is on, or no fries when it is off.

These are two cases of someone inventing a simple two-item code. In one case, the code is: bit on means fries, bit off means no fries, in the other case, bit off means go, bit on means stop. These two bits are the same, they are just used for different purposes, and someone decides what the meaning of these two bits will be. The code is written down somewhere in the law books, or in the restaurant manager's handbook, but the code is not in the bit. The state of the bit merely tells someone which line of the code they are supposed to believe is true at the current moment. That's what a code is.

Like the spies who pass messages by using a secret code, the message may be seen by other people, but those other people don't have the code, so they don't know what the message means. Maybe one spy has a flowerpot sitting on the sill in the front window of his apartment. When the pot is on the left side of the sill, it means "Meet me at the train station at 1:30." And when the flowerpot is on the right side of the sill, it means "No meeting today." Every day, the other spy walks down the street and glances up at that window to see whether he needs to go to the train station today. Everyone else who walks down that street can just as easily see this message, but they don't have the code, so it means nothing to them. Then when the two spies do meet, they can pass a piece of paper that is written in another secret code. They encode and decode the message using a codebook that they do not carry when they meet. So if their message is intercepted by anyone else, it won't mean anything to that someone else. Someone who doesn't have the codebook won't have the proper meanings for the symbols on the sheet of paper.

A computer bit is still, and will always be, nothing more than a place where there is or is not electricity, but when we, as a society of human beings, use a bit for a certain purpose, we give meaning to the bit. When we connect a bit to a red light and hang it over an intersection, and make people study driver's handbooks before giving them driver's licenses, we have given meaning to that bit. Red means 'stop,' not because the bit is capable of doing anything to a vehicle traveling on the road, but because we as people agree that red means stop, and we, seeing that bit on, will stop our car in order to avoid being hit by a car traveling on the cross street, and we hope that everyone else will do the same so that we may be assured that no one will hit us when it is our turn to cross the intersection.

So there are many things that can be done with a bit. It can indicate true or false, go or stop. A single yes or no can be a major thing, as in the answer to "Will you marry me?" or an everyday matter such as "Would you like fries with that?"

But still, there are many things that cannot be done with a bit, or seem to be incompatible with the idea of bits altogether. There can be many examples of yes/no things in everyday life, but there are many more things that are not a simple yes or no.

In the case of the telegraph, which was indisputably just one bit, how can there be more than two items in the Morse code? The answer is that the ability to send and receive messages depended on the skills and the memories of the operators at both ends of the wire. In the Morse Code, if the key was pressed for a very short time, that was called a "dot(.)," and if it was pressed for a slightly longer time, that was called a "dash(-)." Each letter of the alphabet was assigned a unique combination of dots and or dashes, and both operators studied the code, memorized it and practiced using it. For instance, the code for the letter 'N' was dash dot (-.) and the code for the letter 'C' was dash dot dash dot (-.-.). The length of the on times were different to make dots and dashes, and the lengths of the off times were different to distinguish between the time that separates dots and dashes within a letter, the time that separates letters, and the time that separates words. You need a longer off time to keep from confusing a 'C' with two 'N's. The receiving person had to recognize these as patterns – that is, he had to hear and remember the lengths of several on and off times until he recognized a letter. The telegraph apparatus didn't have any memory at all, there was never even one whole letter on the wire at any one time, the pieces of letters went down the wire, to be assembled into dots and dashes in the mind of the operator, then into letters, and then into words and sentences written on a sheet of paper. So the telegraph bit achieves more than two meanings by having several individual times when there may be ons or offs.

If a computer were built on the principles of the Morse code, it would just have a light bulb on top of it flashing the code at us. Since we'd rather see whole letters, words and sentences on the screen simultaneously, we need something more than a single bit and this old code.

Even in the examples used in this chapter, real traffic lights actually have three bits, one for red, one for yellow and one for green. If you had only one bit, you could just have a red light at the intersection, and when it was on that would mean stop, and when it was off that would mean go. But when it was off, you might wonder whether it was really off, or whether the bulb had just burned out. So using three bits is a lot more useful in this case.

In the real world, we have already seen that computers can contain letters, words, sentences, entire books, as well as numbers, pictures, sounds and more. And yet, all of this does come down to nothing more than bits.

If we want our computer memory to be able to hold more than an on or off, or yes or no, we will have to have something more than just one bit. Fortunately, we can do something much more useful just by using several bits together, and then making up a code (or maybe several codes) to assign some useful meaning to them.

A Rose by Any Other Name

Before we go on, we are going to introduce a change to what we call something. As we know, all of the bits in the computer are places where there is or is not, some electricity. We call these states, "on" and "off," and that is exactly what they are. Even though these are short words, there are places where it is a lot easier, clearer and simpler to use a single symbol to describe these states. Fortunately, we're not going to invent anything tricky, we're just going to use two symbols you already know well, the numbers zero and one. From here on out, we will call off 0, and we will call on 1. And sometimes we will still use on and off.

Thus the chart for our NAND gate will look like this:

a	b	c
0	0	1
0	1	1
1	0	1
1	1	0

This is very easy to understand, of course, but the point that needs to be made here, is that the computer parts have not changed, the only thing that has changed is what we, as people looking at the machine, are calling it. Just because we call a bit a zero or one, that doesn't mean that suddenly numbers have appeared and are running around inside the computer. There are still no numbers (or words or sounds or pictures) in a computer, only bits, exactly as previously described. We could have called them plus and minus, yes and no, true and false, heads and tails, something and nothing, north and south, or even Bert and Ernie. But zero and one will do it. This is a just a simple, two item code. On means 1, and off means 0.

As a comment here, there seems to be a trend among the appliance manufacturers of the world to replace the obsolete and old-fashioned terms of on and off with the modern 0 and 1.

On many power switches they put a 0 by the off position, and a 1 by the on position. The first place I saw this was on a personal computer, and I thought that it was a cute novelty, being on a computer, but now this practice has spread to cell phones, coffee makers and automobile dashboards. But I think that this is a mistake. Do you understand that the code could just as easily have been defined as "off means 1 and on means 0?" The computer would work exactly the same way, only the printing in the technical manuals that describe what is happening inside the computer would change.

When you see one of these 0/1 switches, you have to translate it back from this very commonly used computer code into what it really means, on or off. So why bother? You don't want to turn your coffee machine '1', you want the power ON so you can get your java and wake up already. Imagine putting these symbols on a waffle maker back in 1935. Nobody would have had any idea of what it meant. It is probably just so that manufacturers don't have to have switches printed in different languages. Or maybe this trend comes from an altruistic desire to educate the public into the modern 'fact' that a 1 is the same as on, but it isn't a fact, it's an arbitrary code.

Eight Is Enough

In order to be able to represent something more than simple yes/no matters, what we are going to do is to stack up eight bits in a single package, and use them as a single unit. Here is a diagram of how it is done. We have taken eight of our memory bits, each one still has its own data input 'i' and its own output 'o,' but we have wired all eight of the set inputs 's' together. Thus when the single 's' gets turned on and then off again, all eight of these 'M's will capture the states of their corresponding 'i's at the same time. The picture on the left shows all eight 'M's, the one on the right is the same thing, just a little simpler.

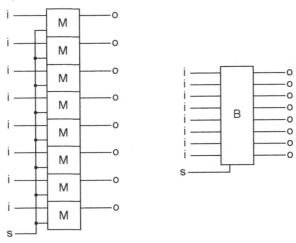

This assembly has a name; it is called a byte, thus the "B" in the diagram. There are several conflicting explanations of exactly where this word came from, but since it sounds just like the word "bite," you can just think of it as a whole mouthful compared with a smaller unit, a bit. Just to show you that computer designers do have a sense of humor, when they use four bits as a unit, they call it a nibble. So you can eat a tiny bit of cherry pie, or have a nibble or take a whole byte.

When we had a bit, we would just say that its state was either 0 or 1. Now that we have a byte, we will write the contents of the byte like this: 0000 0000, and you can see why we switched from using off/on to 0/1. That shows the contents of each of the eight bits, in this case they are all zeros. The space in the middle is just there to make it a little easier to read. The left hand 0 or 1 would correspond to the top bit in our byte, and the rightmost 0 or 1 would represent the bottom bit.

As you had better know by now, a bit has two possible states that it can be in — on or off. If you have two bits, there are four possible states that those two bits can be in. Do you remember the chart we drew for the inputs of the NAND gate? There were four lines on the chart, one for each possible combination of the two input bits to the gate, 0-0, 0-1, 1-0 and 1-1.

Notice that the order of the bits *does* matter – that is, if you look at two bits and only ask how many bits are on, there are only three possibilities: no bits on, one bit on or two bits on. That would be calling the 1-0 and 0-1 combinations the same thing. For the purpose of using multiple bits to implement a code, we definitely care about the order of the bits in a byte. When there are two bits, we want to use all four possibilities, so we have to keep the bits in order.

How many different possibilities are there when you use eight bits? If all you have is one bit, it can be in one of two states. If you add a second bit, the pair has twice as many states as before because the old bit has its two states while the new bit is one way, and then the old bit has its two states while the new bit is the other way. So two bits have four states. When you add a third bit, the first two have four states with the new bit off and four states with the new bit on, for a total of eight states. Every time you add a bit, you just double the number of possible states. Four bits have 16 states, five have 32, six have 64, seven have 128, eight have 256, nine have 512 states, and so on.

We are going to take eight bits, and call it a byte. Since a bit is a thing that has a location in space, that can be in one of two states, then a byte is a thing that has eight separate locations in space, each of which can be on or off, that are kept in the same order. The byte, taken as a whole, is a location in space that can be in any one of 256 states at any given time, and may be made to change its state over time.

Codes

A bit could only represent yes/no types of things, but now that we have 256 possibilities, we can look for things in our lives that are slightly more complicated.

One of the first things that might fit the bill is written language. If you look in a book and see all of the different types of symbols that are used to print the book, you will see all 26 letters of the alphabet in uppercase as well as lowercase. Then there are the numbers 0 through 9, and there are punctuation marks like periods, commas, quotes, question marks, parentheses and several others. Then there are special symbols like the 'at' sign (@,) currency ($,) and more. If you add these up, 52 letters, 10 numbers, a few dozen for punctuation and symbols, you get something like 100 different symbols that may appear printed on the pages of the average book.

From here on out, we will use the word 'character' to mean one of this sort of thing, one of the letters, numbers, or other symbols that are used in written language. A character can be either a letter, a number, a punctuation mark or any other type of symbol.

So we have written language with about 100 different characters, and our byte with 256 possibilities, maybe we can represent language with bytes. Lets see, how do you put an 'A' into a byte? There is nothing inherent in a byte that would associate it with a character, and there is nothing inherent in a character that has anything to do with bits or bytes. The byte doesn't hold shapes or pictures. Dividing a character into eight parts does not find any bits.

The answer, as before, is to use a code to associate one of the possible states of the byte with something that exists in the real world. The letter 'A' will be represented by a particular pattern of 1s and 0s in the bits of a byte. The byte has 256 different possible states, so someone needs to sit down with pencil and paper and list out all 256 of those combinations, and next to each one, put one of the characters that he wants that pattern to represent. Of course, by the time he gets to the 101st line or so, he'll run out of characters, so he can add every type of rarely used symbol he can think of, or he can just say that the rest of the combinations will have no meaning as far as written language is concerned.

And so, in the early days of computers, each manufacturer sat down and invented a code to represent written language. At some point, the different companies realized that it would be beneficial if they all used the same code, in case they ever wanted their company's computers to be able to communicate with another brand. So they formed committees, held meetings and did whatever else they needed to do to come up with a code that they could all agree on.

There are several versions of this code designed for different purposes, and they still hold meetings today to work out agreements on various esoteric details of things. But we don't need to concern ourselves with all that to see how a computer works. The basic code they came up with is still in use today, and I don't know of any reason why it would ever need to be changed.

The code has a name, it is the: American Standard Code for Information Interchange. This is usually abbreviated to ASCII, pronounced "aass-key." We don't need to print the whole code here, but here's a sample. These are 20 of the codes that they came up with, the first 10 letters of the alphabet in uppercase and lowercase:

PART OF ASCII CODE TABLE

A	0100 0001	a	0110 0001
B	0100 0010	b	0110 0010
C	0100 0011	c	0110 0011
D	0100 0100	d	0110 0100
E	0100 0101	e	0110 0101
F	0100 0110	f	0110 0110
G	0100 0111	g	0110 0111
H	0100 1000	h	0110 1000
I	0100 1001	I	0110 1001
J	0100 1010	j	0110 1010

Each code is unique. It's interesting to note the way that they arranged the codes so that the codes for uppercase and lowercase of the same letter use the same code except for one bit. The third bit from the left is off for all uppercase letters, and on for all lowercase letters.

If you wanted to put a message on your computer screen that said "Hello Joe" you would need nine bytes. The first byte would have the code for uppercase "H", the second byte would have the code for lowercase "e", the third and fourth bytes would have the code for lowercase "l", the fifth byte would have the code for lowercase "o", the sixth byte would have the code for a blank space, and bytes seven, eight and nine would contain the codes for "J", "o" and "e."

Notice that there is even a code for a blank space (it is 0010 0000 by the way.) You may wonder why there needs to be a code for a blank space, but that just goes to show you how dumb computers are. They don't really contain sentences or words, there are just a number of bytes set with the codes from the ASCII code table that represent the individual symbols that we use in written language. And one of those "symbols," is the lack of any symbol, called a space, that we use to separate words. That space tells us, the reader, that this is the end of one word and the beginning of another. The computer only has bytes, each of which can be in one of its 256 states. Which state a byte is currently in, means nothing to the computer.

So let us take a memory byte, and set the bits to 0100 0101. That means that we have put the letter E into the byte, right? Well... not really. We have set the pattern that appears next to the letter E in the ASCII code table, but there is nothing inherent in the byte that has to do with an 'E.' If Thomas Edison had been testing eight of his new experimental light bulbs, and had them sitting in a row on a shelf, and the first, third, fourth, fifth and seventh light bulbs had burned out, the remaining light bulbs would be a byte with this pattern. But there wasn't a single person on the face of the Earth who would have looked at that row of bulbs and thought of the letter 'E,' because ASCII had not yet been invented. The letter is represented by the code. The only thing in the byte is the code.

There you have the subject of codes. A computer code is something that allows you to associate each of the 256 possible patterns in a byte with something else.

Another language note here, sometimes the word code refers to the whole list of patterns and what they represent, as in "This message was written with a secret code." Sometimes code just refers to one of the patterns, as in "What code is in that byte?" It will be pretty obvious from the context which way it is being used.

Back to the Byte

Do you remember the memory byte we drew a few chapters ago? It was eight memory bits with their 's' wires all connected together. Almost every time that we need to remember a byte inside a computer, we also need an additional part that gets connected to the byte's output. This extra part consists of eight AND gates.

These eight AND gates, together, are called an "Enabler." The drawing on the left shows all of the parts, the drawing on the right is a simpler way to draw it.

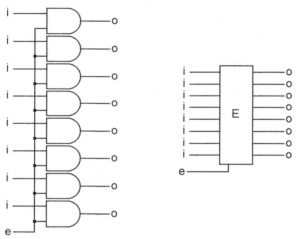

The second input of all eight AND gates are connected together and given the name 'enable,' or 'e' for short. When 'e' is off, whatever comes into the Enabler goes no further, because the other side of each AND gate is off, thus the outputs of those gates are all going to be off. When 'e' is on, the inputs go through the Enabler unchanged to the outputs, 'o.'

By the way, when gates are used for something like this, the name "gate" starts to make some sense. An Enabler allows a byte through when the bit 'e' is 1 and stops the byte when it is 0. So 'e' being on is like opening a gate, and 'e' being off is like closing a gate.

We will take our byte, and connect it to an enabler, as shown in the left hand drawing. To simplify once again, we can draw it as shown on the right.

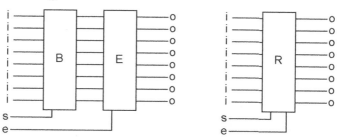

Now we have a combination that can store eight bits. It captures them all at the same time, and it can either keep them to itself, or let them out for use somewhere else. This combination of a Byte and an Enabler, has a name, it is called a Register, thus the 'R' in the drawing.

There will be a few places in this book where there are registers that never need to have their outputs turned off. In those cases, we will draw a register that only has a 'set' bit, and no 'enable' bit. We should probably refer to these devices as 'bytes,' but we will call them registers nonetheless.

Register simply means a place to record some kind of information, like a hotel register where all the guests sign in, or a check register where you write down each check that is written. In the case of this computer part, you record the state of the eight input bits. This register is very limited though, in that it can only hold one set of values; in a hotel register there is a new line for each guest. Every time you store a new state in a computer register, the previous state of the eight memory bits is lost. The only thing that is in there is the most recently saved value.

The Magic Bus

There are many places in a computer where eight wires are needed to connect registers together. Our register, for example, has eight memory bits, each of which have an input and an output. To simplify our diagrams, we will replace our eight wires with a double line.

So our register can look like one of these:

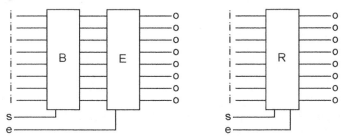

Or, we can simplify, and replace it with one of these:

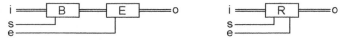

It's exactly the same thing, we will just save a lot of ink in our drawings, and they will be easier to understand.

When there is a connection between two of these bundles of wires, one wire of each bundle is connected to one wire of the other bundle as shown in the diagram on the left. But we will simplify it, and just draw it like the diagram on the right.

Now, this grouping of eight wires is so common inside computers that it has a name. It is called a bus. Why is it called a bus? Well, it probably has to do with the old electrical term 'buss,' that means a bar of metal used as a very large wire in places like power generating plants. But there is also an interesting similarity to the kind of bus that people use for transportation.

A bus is a vehicle that commonly travels along a predetermined route, and makes many stops where people get on or off. They start somewhere, and the bus takes them to some other place they need to be. In the world of computers, a bus is simply a set of eight wires that goes to various places inside the computer. Of course, eight is the number of wires needed to carry a byte of information. Inside the computer, the contents of bytes need to get from where they are to other places, so the bus goes to all these places, and the design of the register allows the contents of any selected byte to get onto the bus, and get off at a selected destination.

In the following example, we have a bus, and there are five registers, each of which has both its input and output connected to the same bus.

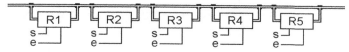

If all of the 's' bits and 'e' bits are off, each register will be set the way it is, and will stay that way. If you want to copy the information from R1 into R4, first you turn the 'e' bit of R1 on. The data in R1 will now be on the bus, and available at the inputs of all five registers. If you then briefly turn the 's' bit of R4 on and back off, the data on the bus will be captured into R4. The byte has been copied. So a computer bus is a little like the bus that carries people. There are a number of stops, and bytes can get to where they need to go.

Notice that we can copy any byte into any other byte. You can copy R2 into R5, or R4 into R1. The bus works in either direction. The electricity put on the bus when you enable any register goes as fast as possible to the inputs of everything else on the bus. You could even enable one register onto the bus and set it into two or more other registers at the same time. The one thing you don't want to do is to enable the outputs of two registers onto the bus at the same time.

In terms of the sizes of bits, you could look at it this way: When the 'e' bit of R1 gets turned on, the bits in R1 now get longer, they are a bigger space because they are now connected to the bus, so those 8 bits now include R1 and the entire bus. When the 's' bit of R4 gets turned on, the R1 bits get even bigger because they now include R1, the bus and R4. If anything in R1 were to somehow change at this time, the bus and R4 would immediately change with it. When the 's' bit of R4 gets turned off, R4 regains its status as a separate byte, and when the 'e' bit of R1 turns off, the bus ceases being a part of R1.

So this is a bus. It is a bundle of eight wires that typically goes to many places.

One more thing about registers: There are many places where we are going to connect the input and output of a register to the same bus, so to simplify even further, we can just show one bundle of wires labeled 'i/o,' meaning input and output. All of the following are exactly equivalent as far as how they work. The placement of the wires on the drawing may be adjusted to make it as uncluttered as possible.

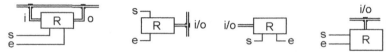

Another language note: A byte is a location that can be in one of 256 states. Sometimes we talk about moving a byte from here to there. By definition, bytes do not move around inside the computer. The byte only refers to the location, but sometimes when someone wants to refer to the current setting of the byte, and they ought to say "lets copy the contents of R1 into R4," they simplify and say "move R1 to R4" or "move this byte over there." They're using the word byte to refer to the contents of the byte. Again, the context usually makes this very clear. In the example above of copying the contents of R1 into R4, you may hear it described as "moving a byte from R1 to R4." Technically, R1 and R4 are the bytes, which do not move, only the contents goes from place to place.

Also, the contents do not leave the place where they came from. When you are done "moving" a byte, the "from" byte has not changed, it doesn't lose what it had. At the other end, the pattern that was originally in the "to" byte is now "gone," it didn't go anywhere, it was just written over by the new information. The old pattern simply ceases to exist. The new information is exactly the same as what is still in the first byte. The byte didn't move, there are still two bytes in two locations, but the information in the first byte has been copied into the second byte.

More Gate Combinations

Now we are going to show just two more combinations, and then we will be able put together what we know so far, to make the first half of a computer. So don't get discouraged, just a little further and we'll be half way home.

The first combination is very simple. It is just an AND gate with more than two inputs. If you connect two AND gates like this diagram on the left, you see that for 'd' to be on, all three inputs, 'a,' 'b' and 'c' have to be on. So this combination can simply be drawn like this diagram on the right:

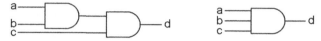

And the chart that shows how it operates looks like this:

a	b	c	d
0	0	0	0
0	0	1	0
0	1	0	0
0	1	1	0
1	0	0	0
1	0	1	0
1	1	0	0
1	1	1	1

Imagine replacing input 'c' with another AND gate, then you would have a four input AND gate. You could then replace any of the four inputs with another AND gate, and have a five input AND gate. This can be done as many times as necessary for what you are doing.

As you add inputs, the chart will need more and more lines. Every time you add another input, you double the number of combinations that the inputs can have. The chart we saw for the original two input AND gate had four lines, one for each possibility. The three input, directly above, has eight lines. A four input AND gate will have 16 lines, a five input will have 32, etc. In all cases though, for an AND gate, only one combination will result in the output turning on, that being the line where all inputs are on.

Here is the last combination we need to make the first half of a computer. This combination is different from anything we have looked at so far, in that it has more outputs than inputs. Our first example has two inputs and four outputs. It is not very complicated, it just has two NOT gates and four AND gates.

In the diagram below, 'a' and 'b' are the inputs coming in from the left. Both of them are connected to NOT gates. The NOT gates generate the opposite of their inputs. There are four vertical wires going down the page that come from 'a' and 'b' and the opposites of 'a' and 'b.' Thus, for each 'a' and 'b,' there are two wires going down the page, where one of them will be on if its input is on, and the other will be on if its input is off. Now we put four AND gates on the right, and connect each one to a different pair of the vertical wires such that each AND gate will turn on for a different one of the four possible combinations of 'a' and 'b.' The top AND gate, labeled "0/0" is connected to the wire that is on when 'a' is off, and the wire that is on when 'b' is off, and thus turns on when 'a' and 'b' are both 0. The next AND gate, "0/1" is connected to the wire that is on when 'a' is off, and 'b,' so it turns on when 'a' is 0 and 'b' is 1, etc.

The inputs can be on in any combination, both bits off, one on, the other on, or both on. None, one or two on. The outputs, however, will always have one and only one output on and the other three off. The one which is on is determined by the current states of 'a' and 'b.'

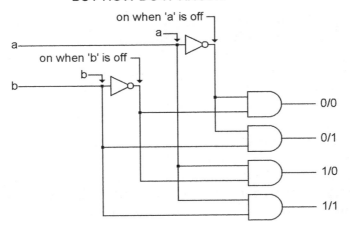

a	b	0/0	0/1	1/0	1/1
0	0	1	0	0	0
0	1	0	1	0	0
1	0	0	0	1	0
1	1	0	0	0	1

This combination is called a decoder. The name means that if you consider the four possible states of the two inputs as a code, then the output tells you which of the codes is currently on the input. Maybe it's not a great name, but that's what it meant to someone once, and the name stuck. This decoder has two inputs, which means that there can be four combinations of the states of the inputs, and there are four outputs, one corresponding to each of the possible input combinations.

This can be extended. If we added a third input, there would then be eight possible input combinations, and if we used eight, three input AND gates, we could build a three input, eight output decoder. Similarly, we could build a four input, 16 output decoder. Decoders are named by the number of inputs "X" the number of outputs. Like 2X4, 3X8, 4X16, 5X32, 6X64, etc.

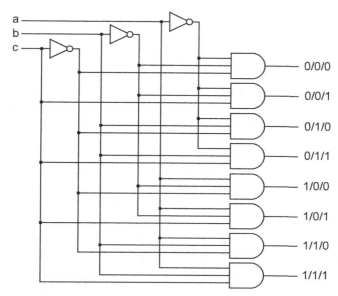

Again, we will simplify our drawings, we won't show any of the internal parts or wiring, we'll just have a box with a name and the inputs and outputs that we are interested in. We have seen how NAND gates make NOT gates and AND gates, and then NOT gates and AND gates make a Decoder. It is a box full of NAND gates wired up to do something useful. We know what it does, one and only one of the outputs is always on, and which one it is, is determined by the state of the three inputs. That's all it does.

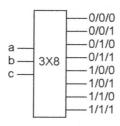

First Half of the Computer

Lets build something with the parts we have so far. Actually, we can now build fully half of what's in a computer.

First, let's build something similar out of wood (in our minds,) then we'll come back and show how to build a computer version that does pretty much the same thing.

You know in a hotel, at the front desk, on the wall behind the clerk, there are a series of little wooden cubbyholes, one for each room in the hotel. That's where they keep extra room keys and messages or mail for the guests. Or you may have seen an old movie where someone in an old post office was sorting the mail. He sits at a table with a series of cubbyholes at the back. He has a pile of unsorted mail on the table, picks up one at a time, reads the address, and puts the letter in the appropriate cubbyhole.

So we're going to build some cubbyholes. Ours will be three inches square, and there will be sixteen cubbyholes high and sixteen cubbyholes across. That's a total size of four feet by four feet, with a total of two hundred fifty six cubbies.

Now we'll add something that they don't have in the post office or the hotel. We're going to put a large wood panel right in front of the cubbies which is twice as wide as the whole thing, and in the middle it has a vertical slot that is just large enough to expose one column of 16 cubbies. The panel will have wheels on the bottom so it can slide left and right to expose any one of the vertical columns of sixteen cubbies at a time, and cover all of the other columns.

Let's take another wood panel just like the first, but turn it up sideways so it is twice as high as our cubbyholes, and the slot in the middle goes side to side. This second panel will be mounted right in front of the first, in something like a window frame, so it can slide up and down, exposing just one row of sixteen cubbies at a time.

So now we have a series of 256 cubbyholes, and two slotted wooden panels in front of them that allow only one cubby at a time to be visible. In each of these cubbies, we will place a single slip of paper on which we will write one of the possible combinations of eight zeros and ones.

This cubbyhole device has 256 places to store something. At any given time, we can select one and only one of those places by sliding the wood panels side to side or up and down. At the selected cubbyhole, we can reach in and get the slip of paper and read it, or replace it with another one.

Now we will take the gates, registers and decoders that we have described, and make something out of them that does pretty much the same thing as our cubbyhole device. This thing will have 256 places in which to store something, and we will be able to select one and only one of those places at any given time.

Referencing the diagram below, we start with a single register. Its input 'a,' is a bus that comes from somewhere else in the computer. A combination of bits is placed on the bus and the 'sa' (set a) bit goes 1 then 0. That bit pattern is now stored in this register, which is one of those registers whose output is always on. The first four output bits are connected to one 4X16 decoder, and the other four output bits are connected to another 4X16 decoder. The outputs of the two decoders are laid out in a grid pattern. The wires do not touch each other, but there are 16 by 16, or 256 intersections here that we will make use of soon. A decoder, as stated, has one and only one of its outputs on at any time, and the rest are off. Since we have two decoders here, there will be one horizontal grid wire on, and one vertical grid wire on. Therefore, of these 256 intersections, there will be only one intersection where both the horizontal and vertical wires are on. Which intersection that is will change every time the value in R is changed, but there will always be one where both wires are on while the other 255 will have only one on or none on.

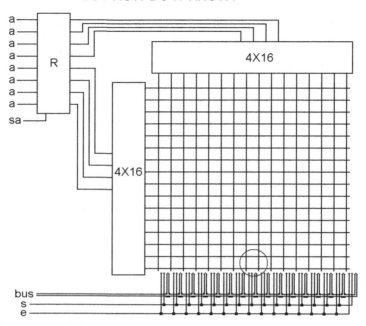

At the bottom of this diagram is one bus and an 's' and 'e' bit, just the same as the connections that go to a register. As you can see, they go upwards and into the grid. The diagram doesn't show it, but they go up under the grid all the way to the top, so that each of the 256 intersections has a bus and an 's' and 'e' bit nearby.

There is a circle on the diagram above, around one of the intersections of the grid. What is in this circle is magnified in the diagram below, showing that there are three AND gates and one register at each of the 256 intersections. As we can see, there is an AND gate 'x,' connected to the one vertical grid wire and the one horizontal grid wire at this intersection. These 'x' gates are the only things connected to the grid. The rest of the connections go down to the bus and 's' and 'e' bits at the bottom of the diagram. Remember that there is only one intersection where both grid wires are on. Therefore, there are 256 of these 'x' gates, but only one of them has its output on at any given time. The output of that 'x' gate goes to one side each of two more AND gates. These two gates control access to the set and enable inputs of the register at that intersection. So when an 'x' gate is off, the 's' and 'e' bits of that register cannot be turned on.

That will be the case for 255 of these registers, the ones where the 'x' gate is off. But one intersection has its 'x' gate on, and its register can be set from the bus, or its contents can be enabled onto the bus and sent elsewhere by using the 's' and 'e' bits at the bottom of the diagram.

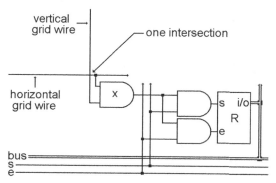

The above is the computer's main memory. It is half of what is necessary to build a computer. It is sometimes called by different names, but the most correct name comes from the fact that you can select any one of the 256 bytes one moment, and then you can immediately select any other of the 256 bytes, and it does not matter where the last one was, or where the next one is, there is no speed advantage or disadvantage to the order in which you select the bytes. Because of this quality, this is a good type of memory to use if you want to be able to access the bytes of memory in a random order. So this type of memory is called "Random Access Memory," or "RAM" for short.

This is RAM. It uses 257 registers. 256 registers are memory storage locations, one register is used to select one of the storage locations and is called the "Memory Address Register" or "MAR" for short. Now that we know what's in it, we can make a simplified diagram like this, and an even simpler bus version:

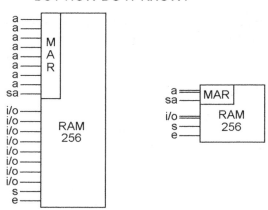

This is fully half of a computer. A computer has just two parts, and this is one of them. So now you know half of what is inside a computer. Every part is made out of NAND gates. That wasn't very difficult was it?

There is one problem here, and that is that 256 bytes is a very small size for a computer's RAM. We may be able to get away with it in this book, but if you want a real computer, it's going to need a RAM with many more bytes to choose from.

A larger RAM can be built by providing two registers that are used to select a memory storage location. This allows the use of 8X256 decoders, and results in a grid with 65,536 intersections, and thus a RAM with 65,536 different locations in which to store something.

Here's an idea of what it would look like: (Don't bother trying to count the grid lines, it was only possible to fit about half of them on the printed page.)

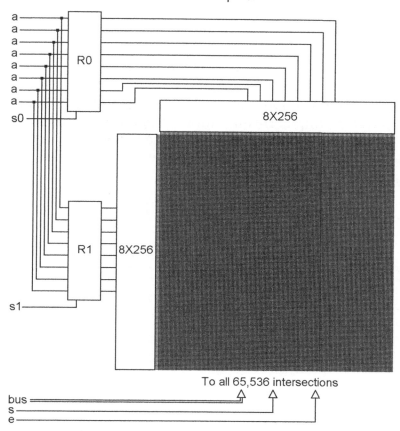

A bus carries one byte at a time, so selecting one of the 65,536 memory locations of this RAM would be a two-step process. First, one byte would have to be placed on the 'a' bus and set into R0, then the second byte would have to be placed onto the 'a' bus and set into R1. Now you could access the desired memory location with the bus and the 's' and 'e' bits at the bottom of the drawing.

Simplifying again, we have something that looks very much like our 256 byte RAM, it just has one more input bit.

```
a ═══╗
s0 ──── MAR
s1 ──── 
i/o ═══    RAM
s ────     65,536
e ────
```

For the rest of this book, we will be using the 256 byte RAM just to keep things simple. If you want to imagine a computer with a larger RAM, every time we send a byte to the Memory Address Register, all you have to do is imagine sending two bytes instead.

Numbers

We are going to return to the subject of codes for a moment. Previously we looked at a code called ASCII that is used to represent written language. Well, numbers are used in written language too, so there are ASCII codes for the digits zero through nine. Earlier we saw 20 of the ASCII codes for part of the alphabet, here are 10 more, the codes for numbers in written language:

0	0011 0000
1	0011 0001
2	0011 0010
3	0011 0011
4	0011 0100
5	0011 0101
6	0011 0110
7	0011 0111
8	0011 1000
9	0011 1001

This is a very useful code, but not everything that computers do has to do with written language. For other tasks, there are other codes that are suited better to those tasks. When it comes to numbers, if you use ASCII, one byte can be any of the 10 digits from 0 to 9. But sometimes there is a byte that is always used to store a number, and that number will never be printed or displayed on the screen. In this case, we can use a different code that doesn't waste any of its possible states on letters of the alphabet or anything other than numbers. Since a byte has 256 possible states, you can have this code represent 256 different numbers. Since we want to include zero, this code starts at zero and goes up to 255.

Now how is this code arranged? The ASCII above is not used at all; this is a completely different code. This code did not require any committee meetings to invent because it is the simplest and most obvious code that computers use. It is the closest thing there is to a 'natural' computer code.

Since this is a long chapter, here is a preview of this code. It consists of assigning a numeric value to each bit in the byte. To use this code, just turn on the bits that add up to the number you want to represent.

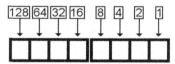

To see how this code works, why it is used in computers, and how those bit values were chosen, we will examine the subject of numbers outside of computers.

There are three number systems that you are probably familiar with that we can analyze. As I see it, these three systems are each made up of two ideas or elements – first, a list of symbols, and second, a method for using those symbols.

Probably the oldest number system around is a simple thing called Tally Marks. It has two symbols, "|" and "/." The method for using these symbols is that you write down a "|" for each of the first four things you are counting, then for the fifth mark, you write a "/" across the first four. You repeat this over and over as long as necessary and then when you're done you count the marks by groups of five – 5, 10, 15, 20, etc. This system is very good for counting things as they pass by, say your flock of sheep. As each animal walks by, you just scratch down one more mark – you don't have to cross out '6' and write '7'. This system has another advantage in that there is actually one mark for each thing that has been counted. Later in the chapter we are going to do some interesting things with numbers that may get confusing, so in order to keep things clear, we will make use of this old system.

Do you remember Roman numerals? It is a number system that also consists of two elements. The first element is the symbols, just selected letters from the alphabet, 'I' for one, 'V' for five, 'X' for ten, 'L' for fifty, 'C' for one hundred, 'D' for five hundred, 'M' for one thousand. The second element is a method that allows you to represent numbers that don't have a single symbol. The Roman method says that you write down multiple symbols, the largest ones first, and add them up, except when a smaller symbol is to left of a larger one, then you subtract it. So 'II' is two (add one and one,) and 'IV' is four (subtract one from five.) One of the things that made this author very happy about the coming of the year 2000 was the fact that Roman numerals representing the year got a lot simpler. 1999 was 'MCMXCIX,' you have to do three subtractions in your head just to read that one. 2000 was simply 'MM.'

The normal number system we use today also consists of two ideas, but these are two very different ideas that came to us through Arabia rather than Rome. The first of these ideas is also about symbols, in this case 0, 1, 2, 3, 4, 5, 6, 7, 8 and 9. These digits are symbols that represent a quantity. The second idea is a method that we are so used to, that we use it instinctively. This method says that if you write down one digit, it means what it says. If you write down two digits next to each other, the one on the right means what it says, but the one to its left means ten times what it says. If you write down three digits right next to each other, the one on the right means what it says, the middle one means ten times what it says and the one on the left means one hundred times what it says. When you want to express a number greater than 9, you do it by using multiple digits, and you use this method that says that the number of positions to the left of the first digit tells you how many times you multiply it by ten before you add them up. So, if you have '246' apples, that means that you have two hundred apples plus forty apples plus six apples.

So how does this work? A number of any amount can be written with the digits zero through nine, but when you go higher than nine, you have to use two digits. When you go above ninety-nine, you have to use three digits. Above nine hundred ninety-nine, you go to four digits, etc. If you are counting upwards, the numbers in any one of the positions go 'round and 'round - zero to nine, then zero to nine again, on and on, and whenever you go from nine back to zero, you increase the digit to the left by 1. So you only have ten symbols, but you can use more than one of them as needed and their positions with regard to each other specify their full value.

There is something odd about this in that the system is based on ten, but there is no single symbol for ten. On the other hand, there is something right about this – the symbols 'o' through '9' do make up ten different symbols. If we also had a single symbol for ten, there would actually be eleven different symbols. So whoever thought of this was pretty smart.

One of the new ideas in this Arabic system was to have a symbol for zero. This is useful if you want to say that you have zero apples, but it is also a necessary thing to keep the positions of the digits straight. If you have 50 apples or 107 apples, you need the zeros in the numbers to know what position each digit is actually in, so you can multiply by ten the correct number of times.

Now these two ideas in the Arabic number system (the digits and the method) have one thing in common. They both have the number ten associated with them. There are ten different digits, and as you add digits to the left side of a number, each position is worth ten times more than the previous one.

In school, when they first teach children about numbers, they say something about our number system being based on the number ten, because we have ten fingers. So here's an odd question: What if this number system had been invented by three-toed sloths? They only have three fingers on each hand, and no thumbs. They would have invented a number system with only six digits- 0, 1, 2, 3, 4 and 5. Could this work? If you had eight apples, how would you write it? There is no number '8' in this system. The answer is, that since the first idea, the digits, was changed to only have six digits, then the second idea, the method, would also have to be changed so that as you add positions to the left, each one would have to be multiplied by sixes instead of tens. Then this system would work. As you count your apples, you would say "0, 1, 2, 3, 4, 5..." and then what?

There's no '6' for the next number. Well, according to the method, when you want to go beyond the highest digit, you go back to '0' and add a '1' to the left. OK, "0, 1, 2, 3, 4, 5, 10, 11, 12." Now you have counted all of your apples. What would this '12' mean? It would be this many: ⵏⵏ. I guess you'd call it eight, but you'd write it '12'. Very odd, but it does work out - 1 times six plus two equals eight apples, it follows the Arabic method, but it is based on six instead of ten. If you continued counting up, when you got to '15,' which is ⵏⵏ (one times six plus five,) the next number would be '20,' but the '2' would mean two sixes, or this many: ⵏⵏ. And 55 would be followed by 100. The '1' in that third position would be how many '36's there were (six times six)

This is a very odd number system, but guess what, you already use it in your everyday life. Yes, think of the way we write time, or the kind of clock that shows the numbers on its face. The right digit of the minutes and seconds follows our normal numbers, 0-9, 0-9, over and over. But the left digit of the minutes and seconds only goes 0-5. After 59 minutes, the clock goes to the next hour and 00 minutes. There are 60 minutes in an hour, numbered from 00 to 59. That left position never gets over 5. That position uses the number system based on six symbols (0-5). The hour part of the clock tells how many '60's there are, though you will never see a 60 on the face of the clock. And you are so used to this that you don't have to think about it. When the clock says 1:30, you know that this is halfway between 1:00 and 2:00, you don't have to do any math in your head to figure it out. Have you ever had to add time? If you add 40 minutes and 40 minutes, you get 80 minutes, but to write that down in hours and minutes, you have to figure out how many 60s there are in 80, in this case 1, then figure out how many minutes there are beyond 60, in this case 20. So you write 1:20. The 1 represents 60 minutes, add 20 and you have your 80 again. So this is pretty complicated, two different number systems in the same number! But you have already been using it your whole life.

| 0-? | 0-5 | 0-9 | 0-5 | 0-9 |

The hour positions are even stranger. On a 12 hour clock, it skips zero and goes 1-12 AM, then 1-12 PM. On a 24 hour clock, it goes from 00-23. We won't try to analyze these. The point we wanted to make was that you are already familiar with number systems based on numbers other than ten.

You could invent a number system for any amount of digits, 10 or 6 like we've seen above, or 3 or 14 or any number you choose. But the simplest one would be if you only had 2 digits, 0 and 1. How would this one work? Well, you'd count 0, 1... and then you're already out of digits – so back to 0 and add 1 on the left, making the next number 10 then 11, then you're out of digits again, so 100 then 101, 110, 111 then 1000. This system is based on two, so there are only two digits, and as you add positions to the left, each one is worth two times more than the previous one. The right position means what it says, the next one to the left means two times what it says, the next means four times what it says, the next means eight times, etc. When you get down to only having two possible digits, you don't have to do much multiplication to figure out the total value of a position. In the position that is worth 'eight,' for example, there can only be a one, meaning one 'eight,' or a zero, meaning 'no eights.'

While we're at it, let's imagine a very strange animal with eight fingers on each hand. That animal would have invented numbers based on sixteen. In their system, they would be able to write ten through fifteen each with a single symbol. Only when they arrived at sixteen would they get back around to 0 and need to put a 1 in the position to the left. To see how this would work, we need six new symbols, so let's just use the first six letters of the alphabet. 'A' will mean ten, 'B' will mean eleven, 'C' will mean twelve, 'D' will mean thirteen, 'E' will mean fourteen and 'F' will mean fifteen. Only after using all sixteen symbols in the right position will we run out of symbols, and the next number will be sixteen, written '10' in this system. If you're familiar with the pounds and ounces system of weights, it's sort of like this system. There are 16 ounces in a pound, so you know that 8 ounces is half a pound. Adding 9 ounces and 9 ounces comes out to 1 pound 2 ounces.

Here is a chart that shows five different number systems. The first column is the old tally mark system to keep it sensible.

Tally	0-9	0-5	0-1	0-F
	0	0	0	0
I	1	1	1	1
II	2	2	10	2
III	3	3	11	3
IIII	4	4	100	4
卌	5	5	101	5
卌 I	6	10	110	6
卌 II	7	11	111	7
卌 III	8	12	1000	8
卌 IIII	9	13	1001	9
卌 卌	10	14	1010	A
卌 卌 I	11	15	1011	B
卌 卌 II	12	20	1100	C
卌 卌 III	13	21	1101	D
卌 卌 IIII	14	22	1110	E
卌 卌 卌	15	23	1111	F
卌 卌 卌 I	16	24	10000	10
卌 卌 卌 II	17	25	10001	11
卌 卌 卌 III	18	30	10010	12

Our normal 0-9 numbers are called the decimal system, because 'dec' means ten in some ancient language. The 0-5 system would be called the senary system, because 'sen' means six in some other ancient language. This new system with just 0 and 1 is called the binary system because 'bi' means two, also because of some ancient language. This other new system, the 0-F system, will be called the hexadecimal system, because 'hex' is another ancient word that means six and 'dec' still means ten, so it's the six plus ten system.

Another method of naming different number systems is to call them by the number they are based on, such as 'base 10' or 'base 2,' etc. meaning decimal or binary, etc. But notice that the number after the word 'base' is written in the decimal system. '2' written in binary is '10,' so 'base 10' would mean binary if the '10' was written in binary. In fact, every number system would be 'base 10' if the '10' was written in that system's numbers! So we could talk about base 2, base 6, base 10 and base 16 if we wanted to, as long as we remember that those base numbers are written in decimal. If we talk about binary, senary, decimal and hexadecimal, it's the same thing, just possibly a little less confusing.

Again, in our normal decimal numbers, the rightmost position is the number of ones. The next position to the left is the number of tens, etc. Each position is worth ten times the previous one. In the binary system, the rightmost position is also the number of ones, but the next position to the left is the number of 'twos,' the next to the left is the number of 'fours,' the next is 'eights.' Each position is worth two times the amount to its right. Since each position has only two possible values, zero or one, this is something that we could use in a byte.

This is the point of this chapter. The binary number system is a 'natural' match to the capabilities of computer parts. We can use it as a code, with off representing zero and on representing one, following the Arabic number method with only two symbols. In a byte, we have eight bits. When we use this code, the bit on the right will be worth 1 when the bit is on, or 0 when it is off. The next bit to the left will be worth 2 when it is on, or 0 when it is off. The next to the left is 4, and so on with 8, 16, 32, 64 and 128. In the order we normally see them, the values of the eight bits look like this: 128 64 32 16 8 4 2 1.

In this code, 0000 0001 means one, 0001 0000 means sixteen, 0001 0001 means seventeen (sixteen plus one,) 1111 1111 means 255, etc. In an eight-bit byte, we can represent a number anywhere from 0 to 255. This code is called the "binary number code."

The computer works just fine with this arrangement, but it is annoying for people to use. Just saying what is in a byte is a problem. If you have 0000 0010, you can call it "zero zero zero zero zero zero one zero binary" or you can mentally translate it to decimal and call it "two," and that is usually what is done. In this book when a number is spelled out, such as 'twelve,' it means 12 in our decimal system. A binary 0000 0100 would be called 'four,' because that is what it works out to be in decimal.

Actually, in the computer industry, people often use hexadecimal, (and they just call it 'hex'.) If you look at the chart above, you can see that four digits of binary can be expressed by one digit of hex. If you have a byte containing 0011 1100, you can translate it to 60 decimal, or just call it "3C hex." Now don't worry, we're not going to use hex in this book, but you may have seen these types of numbers somewhere, and now you know what that was all about.

Addresses

Now that we have the binary number code, we can use it for various purposes in our computer. One of the first places we will use it, is in the Memory Address Register. The pattern of bits that we put into this register will use the binary number code. The bits of this number in MAR then select one of the 256 RAM storage locations. The number in MAR is considered to be a number somewhere between 0 and 255, and thus each of the 256 RAM bytes can be considered to have an address.

This is fairly simple, but a point needs to be made here about exactly what is meant by an address inside of a computer. In a neighborhood of homes, each house has an address, like 125 Maple Street. There is a sign at the corner that says "Maple St." and written on the house are the numerals "125." This is the way we normally think of addresses. The point to be made here is that the houses and streets have numbers or names written on them. In the computer, the byte does not have any identifying information on it or contained in it. It is simply the byte that gets selected when you put that number in the Memory Address Register. The byte gets selected by virtue of where it is, not by any other factor that is contained at that location. Imagine a neighborhood of houses that had sixteen streets, and sixteen houses on each street. Imagine that the streets do not have signs and the houses do not have numbers written on them. You would still be able to find any specific house if you were told, for example, to go to 'the fourth house on the seventh street.' That house still has an address, that is, a method of locating it, it just doesn't have any identifying information at the location. So a computer address is just a number that causes a certain byte to be selected when that address is placed into the Memory Address Register.

The Other Half of the Computer

The other half of the computer is also made ultimately of nothing but NAND gates, and it probably has fewer total parts than the RAM we have built, but it is not laid out so regularly and repetitively, so it will take a little longer to explain. We will call this half of the computer the "Central Processing Unit," or CPU for short, because it does something with and to the bytes in RAM. It "processes" them, and we will see what that means in the next few chapters. The thing that is common to both sides of the computer is the bus.

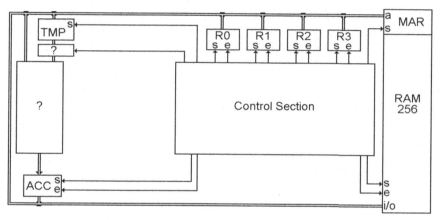

Here are the beginnings of the CPU. The RAM is shown on the right, and the bus makes a big loop between the two bus connections on the RAM. The CPU starts with six registers connected to the bus. These six registers are all of the places that the CPU will use to "process" bytes. That's not so complicated, is it?

The big box labeled "Control Section" in the middle of the diagram will be examined in detail later. It controls all of the 'set' and 'enable' bits in the CPU and the RAM. The boxes with the question marks will be explained immediately following this chapter. For now, we are going to look at where the bytes can go within the CPU.

R0, R1, R2, and R3 are registers that are used as short-term storage for bytes that are needed in the CPU. Their inputs and outputs are connected to the bus. They can be used for many different purposes, so they are known as "general purpose registers."

The register called 'TMP' means temporary. Its input comes from the bus, and its output goes downward to one and then the other of the question marked boxes. TMP has a 'set' bit, but no 'enable' bit because we never have a reason to turn its output off.

The last register is called the accumulator, or ACC for short. This is a word that comes from the days of the old mechanical adding machines (pre 1970.) I guess it meant that as you added up a column of numbers, it would 'accumulate' a running total. In a computer, it just means that it temporarily stores a byte that comes from that big question marked box. The output of ACC is then connected to our old friend, the bus, so it can be sent somewhere else as needed.

The registers in the CPU and RAM are the places where the contents of bytes come from and go to as the computer operates. All movements involve enabling one register onto the bus, and setting the contents of the bus into another register.

Now we will look at what is in those boxes with the question marks.

More Gates

We have used NAND, AND and NOT gates so far. There are two more combination gates that we need to define. The first is built like this:

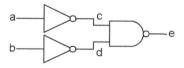

All it does is to NOT the two inputs to one of our good old NAND gates. Here is the chart for it, showing the intermediate wires so it is easy to follow.

a	b	c	d	e
0	0	1	1	0
0	1	1	0	1
1	0	0	1	1
1	1	0	0	1

In this case, when both inputs are off, the output is off, but if either 'a' OR 'b' is on, or both, then the output will be on. So it has another very simple name, it is called the "OR gate." Instead of drawing all the parts, it has its own diagram shaped something like a shield. The diagram and chart look like this:

a	b	c
0	0	0
0	1	1
1	0	1
1	1	1

Like the AND gate, you can build OR gates with more than two inputs. Just add another OR gate in place of one of the inputs, and you will then have three inputs, any one of which will turn the output on. Also like the AND gate, every time you add an input, the number of lines on the chart will double. With the OR gate, only the line that has all inputs off will have the output off. All the rest of the lines will show the output being on.

The last combination gate we need here takes five gates to make, but what it ultimately does is quite simple. Similar to the OR gate, the output is on when either input is on, but in this version, the output goes back off if both inputs are on. So it is called an Exclusive OR gate, or XOR gate for short. The output is on if either OR the other input is on, exclusively. Only if it is OR, not if it is AND. Another way to look it at it is the output comes on if one and only one input is on. Still another way to look at it is the output is off if the inputs are the same, and on if the inputs are different.

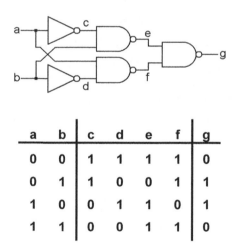

a	b	c	d	e	f	g
0	0	1	1	1	1	0
0	1	1	0	0	1	1
1	0	0	1	1	0	1
1	1	0	0	1	1	0

The simplified diagram looks similar to an OR gate, but it has a double curved line on the input side. The diagram and chart look like this:

a	b	c
0	0	0
0	1	1
1	0	1
1	1	0

We now have four kinds of gates that take two inputs and make one output. They are NAND, AND, OR and XOR. Here is a chart that makes it pretty simple:

a	b	NAND	AND	OR	XOR
0	0	1	0	0	0
0	1	1	0	1	1
1	0	1	0	1	1
1	1	0	1	1	0

For the four possible input combinations of 'a' and 'b,' each type of gate has its own set of output states, and the names of the gates can help you remember which is which.

In spite of the fact that everything in the computer is made out of NAND gates, we are not going to be using any NAND gates by themselves in this computer! Now that we have used them to build AND, OR, XOR and NOT gates, and the memory bit, we are done with the NAND gate. Thank you Mr. NAND gate, bye bye for now.

Messing with Bytes

Individual gates operate on bits. Two bits in, one bit out. But the RAM stores and retrieves a byte at a time. And the bus moves a byte at a time. Here in the CPU, we want to be able to work on a whole byte at one time. We want some 'gates' that affect an entire byte. In the chapter on the bus, we saw how the contents of a byte can be copied from one register to another. This is usually referred to as moving a byte. Now we are going to see some variations on this.

First we will see three ways that we can change the contents of a byte as it moves from one register to another. Second, we will see four ways that we can take the contents of two bytes, and have them interact with each other to create the contents for a third byte. These are all of the things that computers actually do to bytes. All things ultimately come down to these seven operations.

The Left and Right Shifters

The shifter is very easy to build. It doesn't use any gates at all, it just wires up the bus a bit oddly. It is done like this:

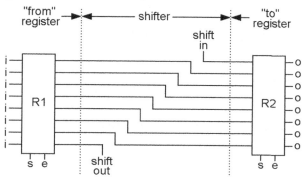

This shows two registers connected by a right shifter. The shifter is just the wires between the two registers. When the 'e' bit of R1 is turned on, and the 's' bit of R2 is turned on and then off, all of the bits in R1 are copied into R2, but they are shifted over one position. The one at the bottom (shift out) can be connected to some other bit in the computer, but is often connected back to the one on the top (shift in) and when that is done, the rightmost bit wraps around to the leftmost bit at the other end of the byte.

A right shifter will change 0100 0010, to 0010 0001.

If 'shift out' is connected to 'shift in,' a right shift will change 0001 1001 to 1000 1100

A left shifter will change 0100 0010 to 1000 0100. The left shifter is wired up like so:

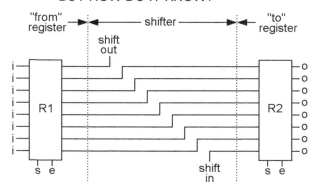

Once again, we have bus versions of these drawings. They each have an 'i' and 'o' bus, and also one input and output bit, like this:

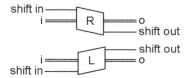

Now of what use is this? The minds of programmers have come up with all sorts of things, but here is an interesting one. Assume that you are using the binary number code. You have the number 0000 0110 in R1. That comes out to the decimal number 6. Now shift that code left into R2. R2 will then be 0000 1100. This comes out to the decimal number 12. What do you know, we have just multiplied the number by 2. This is the basis of how multiplication is done in our computer. How you multiply by something other than 2 will be seen later, but this is how simple it is, just shift the bits. This is similar to something we do with decimal numbers. If you want to multiply something by ten, you just add a zero to the right side, effectively shifting each digit left one position. In the binary system, this only results in multiplying by two because two is what the system is based on.

So that's the shifter, no gates at all.

The NOTter

This device connects two registers with eight NOT gates. Each bit will be changed to its opposite. If you start with 0110 1000, you will end up with 1001 0111. This operation is used for many purposes, the first being in some arithmetic functions. We will see exactly how this works soon after we describe a few other things. Another name for a NOT gate is an "inverter," because it makes the opposite of what you give it, turns it up side down, or inverts it.

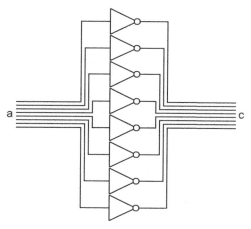

Since the input and the output are both eight wires, we'll simplify by using our bus type picture.

The ANDer

The ANDer takes two input bytes, and ANDs each bit of those two into a third byte. As you can see, the eight bits of the 'a' input bus are connected to the upper side of eight AND gates. The eight bits of the 'b' input bus are connected to the lower side of the same eight AND gates. The outputs of the eight AND gates form the bus output 'c' of this assembly. With this, we can AND two bytes together to form a third byte.

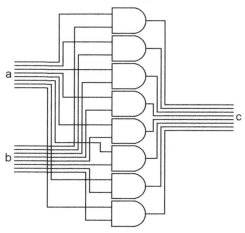

There are many uses for this. For example, you can make sure that an ASCII letter code is uppercase. If you have the code for the letter 'e' in R0, 0110 0101, you could put the bit pattern 1101 1111 into R1 and then AND R1 and R0 and put the answer back into R0. All of the bits that were on in R0 will be copied back to R0 except for the third bit. Whether the third bit had been on or off before, it will now be off. R0 will now contain 0100 0101, the ASCII code for 'E.' This works for all ASCII letter codes because of the way ASCII is designed.

Here is a simpler bus type picture for the ANDer.

The ORer

The ORer takes two input bytes, and ORs each bit of those two into a third byte. As you can see, the eight bits of the 'a' input bus are connected to the upper side of eight OR gates. The eight bits of the 'b' input bus are connected to the lower side of the same eight OR gates. The outputs of the eight OR gates are the bus output 'c' of this assembly. With this, we can OR two bytes together to form a third byte.

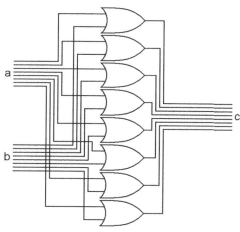

What is the use of this? There are many, but here is one of them. Say you have the ASCII code for the letter 'E' in R0, 0100 0101. If you want to make this letter be lowercase, you could put the bit pattern 0010 0000 into R1 and then OR R0 and R1 and put the answer back into R0. What will happen? All of the bits of R0 will be copied back into R0 as they were except the third bit will now be on no matter what it had been. R0 will now be 0110 0101, the ASCII code for 'e.' This will work no matter what ASCII letter code was in R0 because of the way ASCII was designed.

Here is a simpler bus type picture for the ORer.

The Exclusive ORer

The XORer takes two input bytes, and XORs each bit of those two into a third byte. As you can see, the eight bits of the 'a' input bus are connected to the upper side of eight XOR gates. The eight bits of the 'b' input bus are connected to the lower side of the same eight XOR gates. The outputs of the eight XOR gates are the bus output 'c' of this assembly. With this, we can XOR two bytes together to form a third byte.

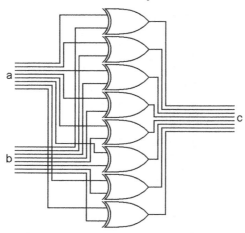

What is the use of this? Again, imaginative people have come up with many of uses. But here is one of them. Say you have one code in R1 and another code in R2. You want to find out if those two codes are the same. So you XOR R1 and R2 into R1. If R1 and R2 contained the same patterns, then R1 will now be all zeros. It doesn't matter what pattern of 0s and 1s was in R1, if R2 contained the same pattern, after an XOR, R1 will be all zeros.

Since both of the inputs and the output are all eight wires, we'll simplify by using our bus type picture.

The Adder

This is a combination of gates that is surprisingly simple considering what it does. In our binary number system, we have numbers in the range of 0 to 255 represented in a byte. If you think about how addition is done with two of our regular decimal numbers, you start by adding the two numbers in the right column. Since the two numbers could each be anywhere from 0 to 9, the sum of these two will be somewhere from 0 to 18. If the answer is anywhere from 0 to 9, you write it down below the two numbers. If the answer is from 10 to 18, you write down the right digit, and carry the 1 to add to the next column to the left.

$$
\begin{array}{c}
2 \\
+4 \\
\hline
6
\end{array}
\qquad
\begin{array}{c}
5 \\
+7 \\
\hline
12
\end{array}
$$

In the binary number system, it is actually much simpler. If you do the same type of addition in binary, the two numbers in the right column can each only be 0 or 1. Thus the only possible answers for adding the right column of two binary numbers will be 0, 1 or 10 (zero, one or two). If you add 0+0, you get 0, 1+0 or 0+1 you get 1, 1+1 you get 0 in the right column, and carry 1 to the column to the left.

$$
\begin{array}{c}
1 \\
+0 \\
\hline
1
\end{array}
\qquad
\begin{array}{c}
1 \\
+1 \\
\hline
10
\end{array}
$$

The gates we have described can easily do this. An XOR of the two bits will tell us what the right column answer should be, and an AND of the two bits will tell us whether we need to carry a 1 to the column on the left. If one bit is on, and the other one is off, that is, we are adding a 1 and a 0, the answer for the right column will be 1. If both numbers are 1, or both numbers are 0, the right column will be 0. The AND gate turns on only in the case where both input numbers are 1.

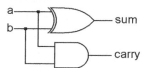

So we have added the right column easily. Now we want to add the next column to the left. Should be the same, right? There are two bits that could be 0 or 1, but this time we also have the possibility of a carry from the previous column. So it's not the same, this time we are really adding three numbers, the two bits in this column, plus the possible carry from the previous column.

Carry-> 0   1   0   1 1

```
   00     01     10      011
  +01    +01    +01     +011
   01     10     11      110
```

When adding three bits, the possible answers are 0, 1, 10 or 11 (zero, one, two or three.) It is more complex, but not impossible. Here is the combination that does it:

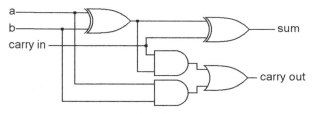

The left XOR tells us if 'a' and 'b' are different. If they are, and 'carry in' is off, or if 'a' and 'b' are the same and 'carry in' is on, then the right XOR will generate 1 as the sum for the current column. The lower AND gate will turn on 'carry out' if both inputs are on. The upper AND gate will turn on 'carry out' if 'carry in' and one of the inputs are on. This is the simplicity of how computers do addition! Now that we see that it works, we can make a simpler picture of it:

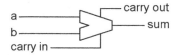

To make an adder that adds two bytes together, we need a one bit adder for each bit of the bytes, with the carry output of each bit connected to the carry input of the next. Notice that every bit has a carry in, even the first bit (the right column.) This is used when we want to add numbers that can be larger than 255.

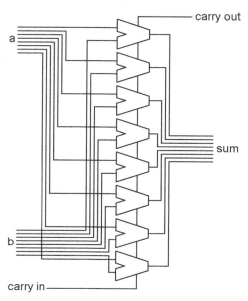

And the simplified picture of it with bus inputs and output:

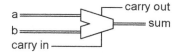

The carry output bit of the leftmost (top) column will turn on if the sum of the two numbers is greater than 255, and this bit will be used elsewhere in the computer.

This is how computers do addition, just five gates per bit, and the computer can do arithmetic!

The Comparator and Zero

All of the things we have described above take one or two bytes as input, and generate one byte of output. The shifters and the adder also generate one extra bit of output that is related to their output byte. The comparator only generates two bits of output, not a whole byte.

The comparator is actually built right into the XORer because it can make use of the gates that are already there. The XORer generates its byte of output, and the comparator generates its two bits. These two functions are not really related to each other, it just happens to be easy to build it this way.

What we want the comparator to do, is to find out whether the two bytes on the input bus are exactly equal, and if not, whether the one on the 'a' bus is larger according to the binary number system.

The equal thing is pretty simple. XOR gates turn off when the inputs are the same, so if all of the XOR gates are off, then the inputs are equal.

To determine the larger of two binary numbers is a little trickier. You have to start with the two top bits, and if one is on and the other is off, then the one that is on is the larger number. If they are the same, then you have to check the next lower pair of bits etc., until you find a pair where they are different. But once you do find a pair that are different, you don't want to check any more bits. For example, 0010 0000 (32) is larger than 0001 1111 (31.) The first two bits are the same in both bytes. The third bit is on in the first byte and off in the second, and therefore the first byte is larger. Although the rest of the bits are on in the second byte, their total is less than the one bit that is on in the first byte.

That is what we want to have happen, and it takes five gates times eight positions to accomplish it. Since we are starting with the XORer, we will add four more gates to each position as shown in this diagram. Remember in the adder, we had a carry bit that passed from the lowest bit position up through to the highest bit. In the comparator, we have two bits that pass down from the highest bit position to the lowest.

Here is one bit of the comparator. You can see the original XOR gate, labeled '1', connected up to one bit of each input bus on the left, and generating one bit for the output bus on the right.

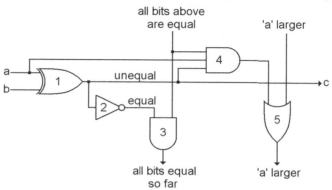

If the output of gate 1 is on, that means that 'a' and 'b' are different, or unequal. We add gate 2, which will turn on when 'a' and 'b' are equal.

If gate 2 is on at every position, then gate 3 will be on at every position as well, and the bit that comes out of the bottom tells us that the two input bytes are equal.

Gate 4 turns on if three things are true. 1) Bits 'a' and 'b' are different. 2) Bit 'a' is the one that is on. 3) All bits above this point have been equal. When gate 4 turns on, it turns gate 5 on, and that turns on every other gate 5 below this point, and therefore the 'a larger' output of the comparator.

When byte 'b' is the larger one, both the 'equal' bit and the 'a larger' bit will be off.

You stack up eight of these bit comparators like the following diagram, with a '1' and '0' connected to the top one to get it started. You still have the XOR function coming out at 'c,' and now the two comparator bits at the bottom.

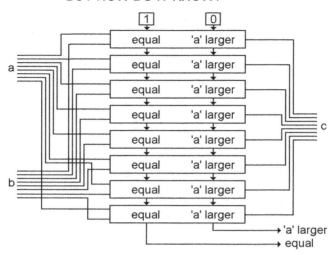

Simplifying again, we will go back to the bus-type XOR diagram, and just add the two new output bits of the comparator.

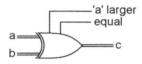

There is one more thing that we are going to need in our computer that gives us another bit of information. This is a simple gate combination that takes a whole byte as input, and generates only one bit as output. The output bit turns on when all of the bits in the byte are off. In other words, the output bit tells us when the contents of the byte is all zeros.

It is simply an eight input OR gate and a NOT gate. When any of the inputs to the OR gate are on, its output will be on, and the output of the NOT gate will be off. Only when all eight inputs of the OR are off, and its output is therefore off, will the output of the NOT gate be on. The simpler bus representation is shown on the right.

Logic

The subject of thinking has been the object of much study and speculation through the ages. There was a man in ancient Greece named Aristotle who did a lot of work in this area. He must have met a lot of illogical people in his life, because he invented a subject that was supposed to help people think more sensibly.

One of his ideas was that if you have two facts, you may be able to derive a third fact from the first two. In school they sometimes give tests that present two facts, then they give you a third fact and ask whether the third fact is 'logical' based on the first two. You may remember questions such as:

If Joe is older than Bill,
And Fred is older than Joe,
Then Fred is older than Bill. True or False?

Or

Children like candy.
Jane is a child.
Therefore Jane likes candy. True or False?

Aristotle called his study of this sort of thing 'Logic.'

The only relevance this has to our discussion of computers is this word 'logic.' Aristotle's logic involved two facts making a third fact. Many of our computer parts, such as AND gates, take two bits and make a third bit, or eight AND gates take two bytes and make a third byte. And so, the things that these gates do, has come to be known as logic. There may be AND logic and OR logic and XOR logic, but the general term for all of them is logic.

ANDing, ORing and XORing take two bytes to make a third, so they fit this definition of logic pretty well. Shifting and NOTing have also come to be known as logic even though they only take one byte of input to generate their output. The ADDer, although it is has two inputs and is also very logical, somehow is not known to be in the category of logic, it is in its own category, arithmetic.

So all of the ways that we have described above of doing things to bytes come under the heading of 'arithmetic and logic.'

The Arithmetic and Logic Unit

Now we have built seven different devices that can do arithmetic or logic on bytes of data. We are going take all seven of these devices, put them together in one unit, and provide a method of selecting which one of these devices we want to use at any given time. This is called the "Arithmetic and Logic Unit,' or "ALU" for short.

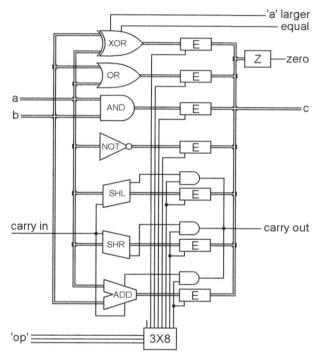

All seven devices are connected to input 'a,' the devices that have two inputs are also connected to input 'b.' All seven devices are connected to the inputs at all times, but each output is attached to one of those enablers. The wires that turn the enablers on, are connected to the outputs of a decoder, thus only one enabler can be on at a given time. Seven of the decoder's outputs enable a single device to continue on to the common output, 'c.' The eighth output of the decoder is used when you don't want to select any device at all. The three input wires to the decoder are labeled 'op,' because they choose the desired 'operation.'

The one little complication here is the carry bits from the adder, and the 'shift in' and 'shift out' bits from the shifters. These are used in very similar ways, and so from here on out we will refer to all of them as carry bits. The adder and both shifters take carry as an input, and generate carry as an output. So the three carry inputs are connected to a single ALU input, and one of the three outputs is selected along with the bus output of its device. Look at the rightmost output of the 3X8 decoder above, and see that it enables both the adder bus and the adder carry bit.

What do we have here? It is a box that has two bus inputs, one bus output and four other bits in and four other bits out. Three of the input bits select which "operation" will take place between the input and output buses. Again, now that we know what's in it and how it works, we don't need to show all of its parts. Here is a simplified way to draw it:

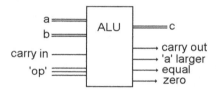

Notice that the three single bit inputs labeled "op," above, can have eight different combinations. Seven of those combinations select one of the devices described previously. The eighth combination does not select any output byte, but the 'a larger' and 'equal' bits still work, as they do at all times, so this is the code to choose if you only want to do a comparison.

The combination of bits at 'op' mean something. That sounds like another code. Yes, here is a three-bit code that we will make use of soon.

000	ADD	Add
001	SHR	Shift Right
010	SHL	Shift Left
011	NOT	Not
100	AND	And
101	OR	Or
110	XOR	Exclusive OR
111	CMP	Compare

The Arithmetic and Logic Unit is the very center, the heart of the computer. This is where all of the action happens. I'll bet this is a lot less complicated than you thought.

More of the Processor

There is one more little device we need. It is a very simple thing, it has a bus input, a bus output and one other input bit. It is very similar to an enabler. Seven of the bits go through AND gates, and one of them goes through an OR gate. The single bit input determines what happens when a byte tries to pass through this device. When the 'bus 1' bit is off, all of the bits of the input bus pass through to the output bus unchanged. When the 'bus 1' bit is on, the input byte is ignored and the output byte will be 0000 0001, which is the number 1 in binary. We will call this device a 'bus 1' because it will place the number 1 on a bus when we need it.

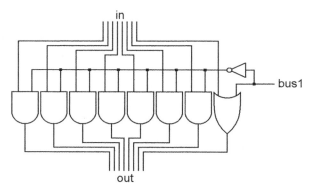

Now we can put this 'bus 1' and the ALU into the CPU. We will change where the wires go in and out of the ALU so it fits our diagram better. The bus inputs come in the top, the bus output comes out the bottom and all of the input and output bits are on the right.

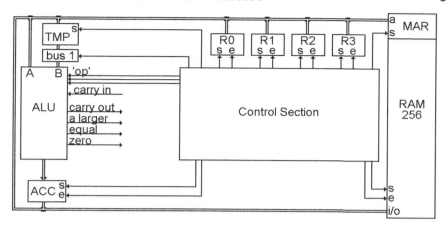

The output of the ALU is connected to ACC. ACC receives, and temporarily stores, the result of the most recent ALU operation. The output of ACC is then connected to the bus, so its contents can be sent somewhere else as needed.

When we want to do a one input ALU operation, we have to set the three 'op' bits of the ALU to the desired operation, enable the register we want onto the bus, and set the answer into ACC.

For a two input ALU operation, there are two steps. First we enable one of the registers onto the bus and set it into TMP. Then we enable the second register onto the bus, choose the ALU operation, and set the answer into ACC.

As you can see, we can now move bytes of data to and from RAM, to and from the Registers, through the ALU to ACC, and from there, into a register or RAM if we turn the appropriate enable and set bits on and off at the right time. This is what happens inside of computers. That's not so complicated, is it?

There is only one thing missing here, and that has to do with all of these control bits on the registers, ALU and RAM. The RAM has three control bits, one to set MAR, one to set the currently selected byte in, one to enable the currently selected byte out. Each of the registers, R0, R1, R2, R3 and ACC have a set and an enable bit, TMP only has a set bit, bus 1 has a control bit, and the ALU has those three 'op' bits that select the desired operation.

We need something that will turn all of these control bits on and off at the appropriate times so we can do something that is useful. Now it is time to look into that box labeled 'Control Section.'

The Clock

We need to turn the appropriate control bits on and off at the appropriate times. We will look at the appropriate bits later, first we will look at the appropriate times.

Here is a new kind of drawing, we will call it a graph. It shows how one bit changes over time. Time starts on the left and marches forward to the right. The line on the graph has two possible positions, up means the bit is on, and down means the bit is off.

This graph shows bit 'X' going on and off, on and off regularly. There could be a time scale on the bottom to show how fast this is happening. If the whole width of the page represented one second, then bit 'X' would be going on and off about eight times per second. But we won't need a time scale in these graphs, as we will only be concerned with the relative timing between two or more bits. The speed in an actual computer will be very fast, such as the bit going on and off a billion times per second.

When something repeats some action regularly, one of those actions, individually, is called a cycle. The graph above shows about eight cycles. You can say that from one time the bit turns on to the next time the bit turns on is a cycle, or you can say that from the middle of the off time to the middle of the next off time is the cycle, as long as the cycle starts at one point in time when the bit is at some stage of its activity, and continues until the bit gets back to the same stage of the activity again. The word 'Cycle' comes from the word 'circle,' so when the bit comes full circle, that is one cycle.

There was a scientist who lived in Germany in the 1800's who did some of the early research that led up to radio. His name was Heinrich Hertz, and among other things, he studied electricity that was going on and off very quickly. Some decades after his death, it was decided to use his name to describe how fast electricity was going on and off, or how many cycles occurred per second. Thus, one Hertz (or Hz for short) means that the electricity is going on and off once per second. 500 Hz means 500 times per second. For faster speeds we run into those ancient languages again, and one thousand times per second is called a kilohertz or kHz for short. Going on and off a million times per second is called a megahertz, or mHz for short, and a billion times is called a gigahertz, or gHz for short.

Every computer has one special bit. All other bits in a computer come from somewhere, they are set on and off by other bits or switches. This one special bit turns on and off all by itself. But there is nothing mysterious about it, it just goes on and off very regularly and very quickly. This special bit is built very simply, like this:

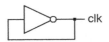

This seems a silly thing to do. Just connect a NOT gate's output back to its input? What will this do? Well, if you start with the output on, the electricity travels back to the input, where it enters the gate which turns the output off, which travels back to the input which turns the output on. Yes, this gate will just go on and off as quickly as possible. This will actually be too fast to be used for anything, and so it can be slowed down just by lengthening the wire that makes the loop.

The simplified diagram shows this to be the one special bit in the computer that has an output but does not have any inputs.

This bit has a name. It is called the clock. Now we usually think of a clock as a thing with a dial and hands, or some numbers on a screen, and we have seen such clocks in the corner of a computer screen. Unfortunately, someone named this type of bit, a clock, and the name stuck with the computer pioneers. It could have been called the drumbeat or the pacesetter or the heart or the rhythm section, but they called it a clock. That is what we will mean when we say clock throughout the rest of this book. I guess it's a clock that ticks, but doesn't have a dial. If we want to talk about the type of clock that tells you what time it is, we will call it a 'time of day clock,' or 'TOD clock' for short. But the word 'clock' will mean this type of bit.

How quickly does this clock go on and off? These days it is well over a billion times per second, or several gigahertz. This is one of the main characteristics that computer companies tell you about to show you how great their computers are. When you see computers for sale, the speed that they advertise is the speed of its clock. The faster a computer is, the more expensive it is, because it can do more things in one second. It is the speed of this single bit going on and off that sets the tempo for the whole computer.

To move data via the bus, we need first to enable the output of one and only one register, so that its electricity can travel through the bus to the inputs of other registers. Then, while the data is on the bus, we want to turn the set bit of the destination register on and off. Since the destination register captures the state of the bus at the instant that the set bit goes off, we want to make sure that it goes off before we turn off the enable bit at the first register to make sure that there are no problems.

Let us first attach a length of wire to the output of the clock. This will delay the electricity slightly. We want it delayed about one quarter of a cycle.

If we show the original clock output (clk) and the delayed clock output (clk d) on a graph, they will look like this:

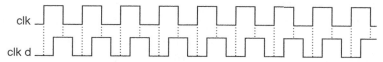

Now we're going to do something fairly simple. We will take the original clock and the delayed clock, and both AND them and OR them to create two new bits, like so:

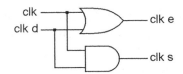

One of the new bits is on when either 'clk' or 'clk d' are on, and the other new bit is on only when both 'clk' and 'clk d' are on. The graph of the inputs and outputs of the AND and OR gates is shown here. They are both still going on and off regularly, but one of them is on for longer than it is off, and the other one is off for longer than it is on. The on time of the second is right in the middle of the on time of the first.

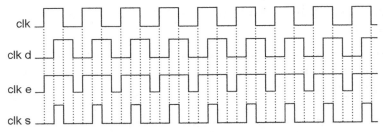

Notice that they have names, 'clk e,' which stands for clock enable, and 'clk s,' which stands for clock set. And what do you know, these two bits have the perfect timing to move a byte of data from one register, across the bus, and into another register. Just connect 'clk e' to the enable bit of the 'from' register, and connect 'clk s' to the set bit of the 'to' register.

Here is a single on/off cycle of these two bits.

If you look at the timing here, this meets our requirements of needing to first enable the output of a register, and then, after the data has a little time to travel down the bus, to turn the set bit of the destination register on and off before turning the enable bit off at the first register.

Of course, these clock bits cannot just be connected directly to every register. There must be other gates in between, that only allow one register to get an enable at any one time, and only the desired register(s) to receive a set. But all enables and sets ultimately come from these two bits because they have the right timing.

Since we will use clk, clk e and clk s throughout the computer, this is the diagram we will use to show the clock:

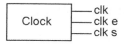

Doing Something Useful

Let's say that we want to do something useful, like adding one number to another number. We have a number in R0, and there is another number in R1 that we want to add to the number in R0. The processor we have built so far has all of the connections to do this addition, but it will take more than one clock cycle to do it.

In the first clock cycle, we can enable R1 onto the bus, and set it into TMP.

In the second cycle we can enable R0 onto the bus, set the ALU to ADD, and set the answer into ACC.

In the third cycle, we can enable ACC onto the bus, and set it into R0.

We now have the old value of R0, plus R1 in R0. Perhaps this doesn't seem very useful, but it is one of the kind of small steps that computers do. Many such small steps make the computer seem to be able to do very complex things.

Thus we see that for the processor to do something useful, it takes several steps. It needs to be able to do actions in a sequence. We need another piece inside this 'Control Section.'

Step by Step

This chapter introduces a new part called the "Stepper." First, we will describe the completed stepper, showing exactly what it does. After that, we will see exactly how it is built. If you happen to trust your author enough to believe that such a stepper can be built out of gates, and you're in such a hurry that you want to skip the 'how it is built' part of the chapter, you might still understand the computer.

Here is a complete stepper.

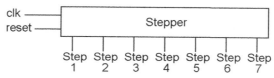

It has two inputs. One is called 'clk,' because this is where we connect a bit that is going on and off, such as our original clock bit. The other input is called 'reset,' which is used to return the stepper back to step one. For outputs, it has a number of bits, each of which will come on for one complete clock cycle, and then turn off, one after the other. The output labeled 'Step 1' turns on for one clock cycle, then 'Step 2' for the next clock cycle, etc. A stepper can be built to have as many steps as needed for any particular task you want to do. In the case of this computer that we are building, seven steps are sufficient. When the last step (7) turns on, it stays on, and the stepper doesn't do anything else until the reset bit is turned on briefly, at which time the steps start over again beginning with 'Step 1.'

Here is a graph of the input 'clk' bit, and the outputs of a seven-step stepper.

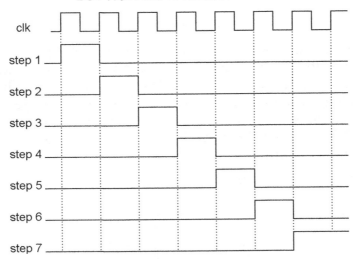

Here is how the stepper is built. It is done using some of the same memory bits that we used to make registers, but they are arranged very differently. We are not going to store anything in these bits, we are going to use them to create a series of steps.

The stepper consists of several memory bits connected in a string, with the output of one connected to the input of the next. Here is a diagram that shows most of the stepper:

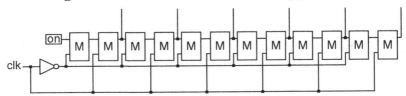

First look at the series of 'M' memory bits just like the ones that we used earlier in the book. In this picture, there are twelve of them connected together, with the output of one connected to the input of the next, all the way down the line. The input to the first bit on the left is connected to a place where the electricity is always on, so when the set bit of that 'M' comes on, that 'M' will receive that on state, and pass it through to its output.

If you look at the set bits of these 'M's, you will see that the set bits of the even numbered 'M's are connected to clk, and the set bits of the odd numbered 'M's are connected to the same clock after it goes through a NOT gate. This new bit that is made by passing clk through a NOT gate can be called 'not clk,' and we can show both on this graph:

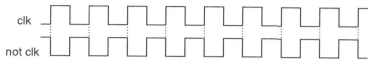

So what will happen with this bunch of gates? If you assume that all of the 'M's start in the off state, and then start 'clk' "ticking," here is what it will do.

The first time 'clk' comes on, nothing will happen, because the set bit of the first 'M' is connected to 'not clk,' which is off when 'clk' is on. When 'clk' goes off, 'not clk' turns on, and the first 'M' will come on, but nothing will happen at the second 'M' because its 'set' bit is connected to 'clk,' which is now off. When 'clk' comes back on, the second 'M' will now come on. As the clock ticks, the 'on' that enters the first memory bit will step down the line, one bit for each time the clock goes on, and one bit for each time the clock goes off. Thus two bits come on for each clock cycle.

Now, turning to the full stepper diagram below, step 1 comes from a NOT gate connected to the output of the second 'M.' Since all 'M's start off, step 1 will be on until the second 'M' comes on, at which time step 1 will be over. For the remaining steps, each one will last from the time its left side 'M' turns on until the time its right side 'M' turns on. The AND gates for steps 2-6 have both inputs on when the left 'M' is on, and the right 'M' is off. If we connect the output of one 'M' and the NOT of the output of an 'M' two spaces farther on to an AND gate, its output will be on for one complete clock cycle. Each one comes on when its left input has come on, but its right input has not yet come on. This gives us a series of bits that each come on for one clock cycle and then turn off.

The only thing missing here is that the 'M' bits come on and stay on. Once they are all on, there is no more action despite the clock's continued ticking. So we need a way to reset them all off so we can start over again. We have to have a way to turn off the input to the first 'M,' and then turn on all of the set bits at the same time. When that happens, the 'off' at the input to the first

'M' will travel through all of the 'M's as fast as it can go. We will add a new input called 'reset,' which will accomplish these things.

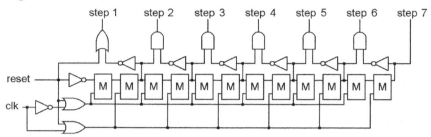

When we turn 'reset' on, it makes the input to the first 'M' bit a zero, and turns on all of the 'sets' at the same time so that the zero can travel down the line of 'M's very quickly. Reset is also ORed with step 1 so that step 1 turns on immediately. Now all of the bits are off, and we have started another sequence. Reset only needs to be turned on for a fraction of one clock cycle.

To recap, this is a stepper. It has two inputs: a clock and a reset. For outputs, it has a number of bits, each of which will come on for one clock cycle. We can actually make this as long as needed, but for the purposes of this book, a seven stage stepper will be sufficient. There will be only one stepper in our computer, we will represent it with this simplified diagram.

We have relocated the Reset bit to the right side of the diagram, and connected it to the last step (7,) so that the stepper will automatically reset itself. Step 7 will not be on for very long, however, because it shuts itself off as soon as the zero can get through the string of 'M's. This means that step 7 will not last long enough to be used for one of our data transfers over the bus. All of the things we want to accomplish will take place in steps 1 through 6.

Everything's Under Control

With our clock, we have a drumbeat to make things go. It has a basic output, and two more that are designed to facilitate the movement of the contents of registers from one to another. With the stepper, we have a series of bits that come on one after another, each for one clock cycle.

Remember the diagram of the CPU we saw a few chapters back? It showed the bus, the ALU, six registers and even the other half of the computer (the RAM) all connected up pretty neatly. At least all of the bus connections were there. But all the registers, the RAM, the Bus 1 and the ALU are controlled by wires that come from that mysterious box labeled 'Control Section' that we know nothing about yet. Now it is time to look inside that box.

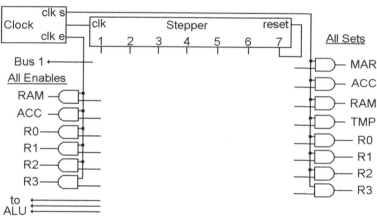

This drawing is the beginning of the control section of the computer. At the top are the clock and the stepper. Then all of the control bits from the registers and RAM have been brought here together in one place, with all of the 'enable' bits on the left, and all of the 'set' bits on the right. Then we have connected the output of an AND gate to each 'enable' and each 'set' bit. One input of each AND gate is connected to either 'clk e' for the 'enables' on the left, or 'clk s' for the 'sets' on the right. Thus, if we use the other input of those AND gates to select any of those registers, the 'enable' bit of all of the items on the left will never be turned on except during 'clk e' time. Similarly on the right, the 'set' bit of any of those registers will only be turned on during 'clk s' time.

This is sort of a switchboard. Everything we need to make the computer do something is right here in one place. All we need to do is connect some control bits to some steps in an intelligent manner, and something useful will happen.

Doing Something Useful, Revisited

Now that we have the beginning of our control section, we can just add a few wires, and we will be able to do the simple addition we postulated earlier, that of adding R1 to R0.

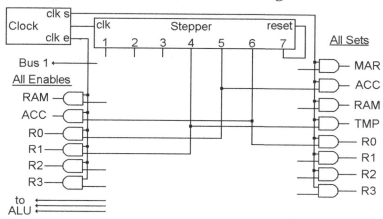

All we have to do to 'do something useful,' like adding R1 to R0, is to connect a few wires in the middle, as shown in this diagram with steps four, five and six. Each step causes something to happen to some of the parts that are shown in the CPU diagram. Each step is connected to one 'enable' on the left, and one 'set' on the right, and therefore causes one part to connect its output to the bus, and another part to save what now appears at its input. Step four is wired to R1 'enable' and TMP 'set.' Step five is wired to R0 'enable,' and ACC 'set.' The ALU 'op' bits do not need any connections since the 'op' code for ADD is 000. Step six is wired to ACC 'enable' and R0 'set.'

During step four, R1 is enabled and TMP is set. The contents of R1 travel across the bus (in the CPU diagram) and are captured by TMP.

During step five, R0 is enabled and ACC is set. If we wanted to do something other than ADD, this is the step where we would turn on the appropriate ALU 'op' code bits.

During step six, ACC is enabled and R0 is set.

Here is a graph of the steps, showing when each register gets enabled and set.

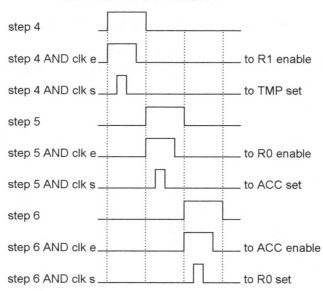

step 4

step 4 AND clk e — to R1 enable

step 4 AND clk s — to TMP set

step 5

step 5 AND clk e — to R0 enable

step 5 AND clk s — to ACC set

step 6

step 6 AND clk e — to ACC enable

step 6 AND clk s — to R0 set

R0 now contains the sum of the original contents of R0 plus R1.

This is how the computer makes things happen in a tightly controlled ballet of bits and bytes moving around inside the machine.

In step seven, the stepper is reset to step 1, where the process repeats. Of course it is not very useful to just do this addition over and over again, even if you start out with the number 1 in both R0 and R1, R0 will get up to 255 pretty quickly.

If the clock in our computer ticks one billion times every second, otherwise known as one gigahertz, and even if we use multiple clock cycles to "do something useful" like this, that means that the computer can do something like this hundreds of millions of times in one second. But we don't want to just add R1 to R0 over and over again.

Perhaps now that we have added R1 to R0, we want to store that new number to a particular address in RAM, and R2 happens to have that address in it. Again, our processor has all of the connections necessary to do this, and again it will take more than one clock cycle to do it. In step 4, we can move R2 across the bus to MAR. In step 5 we can move R0 across the bus to

RAM. That's all that is needed, just two clock cycles and we're done.

The wiring for this operation is simpler than the other one, just two enables and two sets.

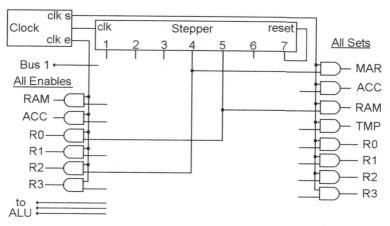

There are many combinations of things that we can do with the RAM, the six registers and the ALU. We could get a byte from RAM and move it to any of the four registers, we could move any one or two of the registers through the ALU and ADD them, AND them, OR them, XOR them, etc.

We need a way for our CPU to do one thing one time, and a different thing the next time. The control section needs something to tell it what to do in each sequence.

What's Next?

Now here's a scary idea. Imagine that the job that an employee does at a fast food restaurant gets broken down into its individual elements. Walk to the counter, say "May I take your order?" listen to the answer, press the "cheeseburger" button on the cash register, etc. Now lets say that there are 256 or less individual actions involved in the job of working at such an establishment. You could then invent a code that would associate one of the states of a byte with each of the individual activities of an employee. Then you could express the sequence of an employee's actions as a sequence of bytes.

First we make up a code table. We write some codes down the left side of the page. Then we decide what we want those codes to mean, and write those meanings next to the codes. Now we have a list of all of the possible actions that an employee might take, and a code that represents each one of them:

```
0000 0000 = Walk to the counter
0000 0001 = Say "May I take your order?"
0000 0010 = Listen to the answer
0000 0011 = Press the cheeseburger button
0000 0100 = Press the fries button.
0000 0101 = Press the milk button
0000 0110 = Press the total button
0000 0111 = Collect the money
0000 1000 = Give the customer the change
0000 1001 = Open an empty bag
0000 1010 = Place a cheeseburger in the bag
0000 1011 = Place fries in the bag
0000 1100 = Place a milk container in the bag
0000 1101 = Hand the bag to the customer
1000 0000 = Go to the step number in the right 6 bits.
0100 0000 = If "yes," go to the step number in the right 6 bits.
0001 0000 = Go home.
```

Now if we want to describe how the employee is supposed to act, we write a sequence of events that he should follow:

```
1.  0000 0000 = Walk to the counter.
2.  0000 0001 = Say "May I take your order?"
3.  0100 0010 = If customer is not answering, go to step 2.
4.  0000 0010 = Listen to the answer.
```

5. 0100 0111 = If customer doesn't say cheeseburger, go to step 7.
6. 0000 0011 = Press the cheeseburger button.
7. 0100 1001 = If customer does not say fries, go to step 9.
8. 0000 0100 = Press the fries button.
9. 0100 1011 = If customer does not say milk, go to step 11.
10. 0000 0101 = Press the milk button.
11. 0100 1101 = If the customer says that's all, go to step 13.
12. 1000 0100 = Go back to step 4.
13. 0000 0110 = Press the total button.
14. 0000 0111 = Collect the money.
15. 0000 1000 = Make change and give it to the customer.
16. 0000 1001 = Open an empty bag.
17. 0101 0011 = If order doesn't include cheeseburger, go to step 19.
18. 0000 1010 = Place a cheeseburger in the bag.
19. 0101 0110 = If order does not include fries, go to step 22.
21. 0000 1011 = Place fries in the bag.
22. 0101 1000 = If order does not include milk, go to step 24.
23. 0000 1100 = Place a milk container in the bag.
24. 0000 1101 = Hand the bag to the customer.
25. 0101 1011 = If it is quitting time, go to step 27.
26. 1000 0001 = Go back to step 1.
27. 0001 0000 = Go home.

I hope nobody ever tries to make the employees of a fast food restaurant learn a code like this. People don't take well to being so mechanized. But maybe someone will try to staff one of these restaurants with robots someday. In that case, the robots would probably work better using this sort of a code.

And our computer might be able to 'understand' a code like this.

The First Great Invention

What we need is some way to do different operations from one stepper sequence to the next. How could we have it wired up one way for one sequence, and then a different way for the next sequence? The answer, of course, is to use more gates. The wiring for one operation can be connected or disconnected with AND gates, and the wiring for a different operation can be connected or disconnected with some more AND gates. And there could be a third and fourth possibility or more. As long as only one of those operations is connected at one time, this will work fine. Now we have several different operations that can be done, but how do you select which one will be done?

The title of this chapter is "The First Great Invention," so what is the invention? The invention is that we will have a series of instructions in RAM that will tell the CPU what to do. We need three things to make this work.

The first part of the invention is, that we are going to add another register to the CPU. This register will be called the "Instruction Register," or "IR" for short. The bits from this register will "instruct" the CPU what to do. The IR gets its input from the bus, and its output goes into the control section of the CPU where the bits select one of several possible operations.

The second part of the invention is another register in the CPU called the "Instruction Address Register," or "IAR" for short. This register has its input and output connected to the bus just like the general purpose registers, but this one only has one purpose, and that is to store the RAM address of the next instruction that we want to move into the IR. If the IAR contains 0000 1010 (10 decimal,) then the next instruction that will be moved to the IR is the byte residing at RAM address ten.

The third part of the invention is some wiring in the control section that uses the stepper to move the desired "instruction" from RAM to the IR, add 1 to the address in the IAR and do the action called for by the instruction that has been put in the IR. When that instruction is complete, the stepper starts over again, but now the IAR has had 1 added to it, so when it gets that instruction from RAM, it will be a different instruction that was located at the following RAM address.

The result of these three parts is a great invention. This is what allows us to make the computer do many different things. Our bus, ALU, RAM and registers make many combinations possible. The contents of the IR will determine what registers are sent to where, and what kind of arithmetic or logic will be done upon them. All we have to do is to place a series of bytes in RAM that represent a series of things that we want to do, one after another.

This series of bytes residing in RAM that the CPU is going to make use of is called a "program."

The basic thing that happens here is that the CPU "fetches" an instruction from RAM, and then "executes" the instruction. Then it fetches the next one and executes it. This happens over and over and over, millions or billions of times every second. This is the simplicity of what a computer does. Someone puts a program in RAM, and that program, if intelligently designed, makes the computer do something that people find useful.

The stepper in this computer has seven steps. The purpose of step 7 is only to reset the stepper back to step 1. So there are six steps during which the CPU does small things. Each step lasts for one clock cycle. The six steps taken as a whole is called an "Instruction Cycle." It takes six steps for the CPU to do all of the actions necessary to fetch and execute one instruction. If we assume that our clock ticks at one gigahertz, then our computer will be able to execute 166,666,666 instructions every second.

Here is the picture of the CPU with the two new registers added to it. There they are under the Control Section, connected to the bus. The IAR has a 'set' and 'enable,' the IR only has a 'set,' just like TMP and MAR because their outputs are not connected to the bus, so we never need to turn them off.

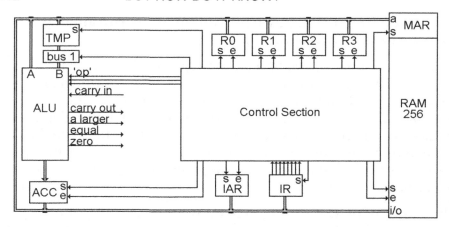

Below is the wiring within the Control Section that does the 'fetch' part of the instruction cycle. It uses the first three steps of the stepper and is the same for all types of instructions.

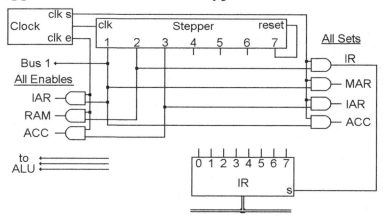

The stepper's first three steps are shown here, and result in 'fetching' the next 'instruction' from RAM. Then the rest of the steps 'execute' the 'instruction.' Exactly what will be done in steps 4, 5 and 6, is determined by the contents of the instruction that was fetched. Then the stepper starts over, fetches the next instruction, and executes it.

The bottom of this diagram includes the Instruction Register. Notice that we have given numbers to the individual bits of the IR, 0 at the left through 7 on the right. We will be referring to the individual bits soon.

Here are the details of exactly how steps 1, 2 and 3 result in fetching an instruction in our little computer:

Step 1 is the most complicated because we actually accomplish two things at the same time. The main thing we want to do is to get the address in IAR over to MAR. This is the address of the next instruction that we want to fetch from RAM. If you look at the wire coming out of step 1 of the stepper, you can see that two of the places it is connected to are the 'enable' of IAR and the 'set' of MAR. Thus, the contents of IAR will be placed on the bus during 'clk e' and set into MAR during 'clk s.' Sometime during the instruction cycle, we need to add 1 to the value in IAR, and since IAR is already on the bus, we might as well do it now. If we don't send anything to the ALU's 'op' bits, they will all be zero, and since 000 is the code for ADD, the ALU will be doing an ADD operation on whatever is on its two inputs, and presenting the answer to ACC. One input comes from the bus, which has IAR on it during this time. If we also turn on the 'bus 1' bit during step 1, the other input to the ALU will be a byte with the binary value of 1. If we turn on the 'set' of ACC during 'clk s,' we will capture the sum of IAR plus 1 in ACC. This just happens to be the address of the instruction that we will want to fetch after we are done with the current one!

Step 2 enables the currently selected byte in RAM onto the bus, and sets it into IR. This is the instruction that we will 'execute' in steps 4, 5 and 6 of this instruction cycle. In the diagram, you can see that the wire coming from step 2 is connected to the 'enable' of RAM and the 'set' of IR.

In step 3, we need to finish updating IAR. We added 1 to it in step 1, but the answer is still in ACC. It needs to be moved to IAR before the beginning of the next instruction cycle. So you can see the wire coming out of step 3 is connected to 'enable' of ACC and 'set' of IAR.

By the time we get to step 4, the instruction has already been moved from RAM to IR, and now steps 4, 5 and 6 can then do whatever is called for by the contents of IR. When that operation is done and the stepper is reset, the sequence will start over again, but now IAR has had 1 added to it, so the instruction at the next RAM address will be fetched and executed.

This idea of putting a series of instructions in RAM and having the CPU execute them is a great invention.

Instructions

We now have this new register, called the Instruction Register, which contains a byte that is going to tell the Control Section what to do. The patterns that are put into this register have a meaning. Sounds like another code, and indeed, it is. This code will be called the "Instruction Code."

Since we are building this computer from scratch, we get to invent our own instruction code. We will take the 256 different codes that can be put in the Instruction Register, and decide what they will mean. Then we have to design the wiring inside the control unit that will make these instructions do what we said they would do.

Do you remember the binary number code? We said that it was the closest thing to a 'natural' computer code because it was based on the same method we use for our normal number system. Then there was the ASCII code, which was just invented by a bunch of people at a meeting. There is nothing natural about ASCII at all, it was just what those people decided it would be.

Now we have the Instruction Code, which will also be a totally invented code - nothing natural about it. Many different instruction codes have been invented for many different types of computers. We will not study any of them here, nor will you need to study any of them later, unless you are going to go on to a highly technical career where that is necessary. But all Instruction Codes are similar, in that they are what make the computer work. The only Instruction Code in this book will be one that we invent for our simple computer. The most important thing in inventing our Instruction Code, will be how simple we can make the wiring that will make the code work.

How many different instructions could there be? Since the instruction register is a byte, there might be as many as 256 different instructions. Fortunately, we will only have nine types of instructions, and all 256 combinations will fall into one of these categories. They are pretty easy to describe.

All instructions involve moving bytes across the bus. The
instructions will cause bytes to go to or from RAM, to or from
registers, and sometimes through the ALU. In the following
chapters, for each type of instruction, we will look at the bits of
that instruction, the gates and wiring necessary to make it work,
and another handy code we can use to make writing programs
easier.

The Arithmetic or Logic Instruction

This first type of instruction is the type that uses the ALU like our ADD operation earlier. As you recall, the ALU has eight things it can do, and for some of those things it uses two bytes of input, for other things it only uses one byte of input. And in seven of those cases, it has one byte of output.

This type of instruction will choose one of the ALU operations, and two registers. This is the most versatile instruction that the computer can do. It actually has 128 variations, since there are eight operations, and four registers, and you get to choose twice from the four registers. That is eight times four times four, or 128 possible ways to use this instruction. Thus this is not just one instruction, but rather it is a whole class of instructions that all use the same wiring to get the job done.

Here is the Instruction Code for the ALU instruction. If the first bit in the Instruction Register is a 1, then this is an ALU instruction. That's the simplicity of it. If the first bit is on, then the next three bits in the instruction get sent to the ALU to tell it what to do, the next two bits choose one of the registers that will be used, and the last two bits choose the other register that will be used.

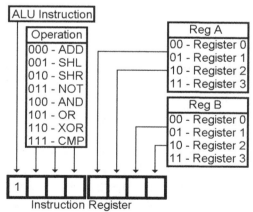

Instruction Register

Therefore, the ALU Instruction (1), to add (000) Register 2 (10) and Register 3 (11), and place the answer in Register 3, would be: 1000 1011. If you placed this code (1000 1011) in RAM at address 10, and set the IAR to 10, and started the computer, it would fetch the 1000 1011 from address 10, place it in IR, and then the wiring in the control section would do the addition of R2 and R3.

If you choose a one input operation, such as SHL, SHR or NOT, the byte will come from the Reg A, go through the ALU, and the answer will be placed in the Reg B. You can choose to go from one register to another such as R1 to R3, or choose to go from one register back into the same one, such as R2 to R2. When you do the latter, the original contents of the register will be replaced.

For two input operations, Reg A and Reg B will be sent to the ALU, and the answer will be sent to Reg B. So whatever was in Reg B, which was one of the inputs to the operation, will be replaced by the answer. You can also specify the same register for both inputs. This can be useful, for instance, if you want to put all zeros in Register 1, just XOR R1 with R1. No matter what is in R1 to begin with, all bit comparisons will be the same, which makes the output of all bits zeros, which gets placed back into R1.

The CMP operation takes two inputs and compares them to see if they are equal, and if not, if the first one is larger. But the CMP operation does not store its output byte. It does not replace the contents of either input byte.

The wiring in the Control unit for the ALU instruction is pretty simple, but there is one extra thing that will be used by many types of instructions that we need to look at first. This has to do with the registers. In "Doing Something Useful Revisited," we used two registers. To use them, we just connected the AND gate for each register to the desired step of the stepper. This was fine, but in the ALU instruction, and many others, there are bits in the instruction register that specify which register to use. Therefore we don't want to wire up directly to any one register, we need to be able to connect to any of the registers, but let the bits in the instruction choose exactly which one. Here is the Control Section wiring that does it:

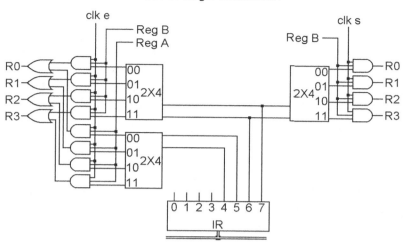

Look at the right side first. When we want to set a general-purpose register, we connect the proper step to this wire that we will call 'Reg B.' As you can see, 'clk s' is connected to all four AND gates. 'Reg B' is also connected to all four AND gates. But these four AND gates each have three inputs. The third input to each AND gate comes from a 2x4 decoder. You remember that one and only one output of a decoder is on at any given time, so only one register will actually be selected to have its 'set' bit turned on. The input to the decoder comes from the last two bits of the IR, so they determine which one register will be set by this wire labeled 'Reg B.' If you look back at the chart of the bits of the ALU Instruction Code, it shows that the last two bits of the instruction are what determine which register you want to use for Reg B.

The left side of the picture is very much like the right side, except that there are two of everything. Remember that in an ALU instruction such as ADD, we need to enable two registers, one at a time, for the inputs to the ALU. The last two bits of the instruction are also used for 'Reg B' on the left, and you can see that 'clk e,' 'Reg B' and a decoder are used to enable one register during its proper step. Bits 4 and 5 of the IR are used to enable 'Reg A' during its proper step, using a separate decoder and a wire called 'Reg A.' The outputs of these two structures are ORed together before going to the actual register enable bits. We will never select 'Reg A' and 'Reg B' at the same time.

What happens when the instruction that has been fetched begins with a 1? That means that this is an ALU instruction, and we need to do three things. First we want to move 'Reg B' to TMP. Then we want to tell the ALU which operation to do, put 'Reg A' on the bus and set the output of the ALU into ACC. Then we want to move ACC to 'Reg B.'

Bit 0 of the IR is the one that determines if this is an ALU instruction. When Bit 0 is on, the things that Bit 0 is wired up to make all of the steps of an ALU instruction occur.

The next diagram shows the eight gates and the wires that are added to the Control Section that make steps 4, 5 and 6 of an ALU instruction do what we need them to do.

In the diagram below, just above and to the left of the IR, there are three AND gates. The outputs of these gates go to the three 'op' wires on the ALU that tell it which operation to do. Each of these three AND gates has three inputs. One input of each gate is wired to bit 0 of the IR. A second input of each gate is wired to step 5 from the stepper. The remaining input of each gate is wired to bits 1, 2 and 3 of the IR.

Therefore, the three wires that go to the ALU will be 000 at all times except during step 5 when IR bit 0 happens to be a 1. At such a time, the wires going to the ALU will be the same as bits 1, 2 and 3 of the IR.

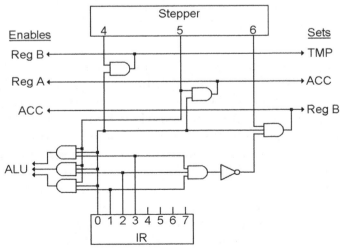

IR bit 0 continues up the diagram, turns right and is connected to one side of three more AND gates. The other sides of these gates are connected to Steps 4, 5 and 6.

The output of the first gate comes on during step 4, and you can see it going to two places. On the left, it enables 'Reg B' onto the bus, and on the right, it sets the bus into TMP. This step is actually not necessary for the SHL, SHR and NOT operations, but it doesn't harm anything, and it would be fairly complicated to get rid of, so for simplicity's sake we'll just leave it this way.

The second gate comes on during step 5 (the same step that the ALU gets its orders), and going to the left is a wire that enables 'Reg A' onto the bus. The ALU now has one input in TMP, the other input on the bus, and its operation specified by those three 'op' wires, so on the right is a wire that sets the answer into ACC.

The third gate turns on during step 6. The wire going to the left enables ACC onto the bus, and the wire going to the right sets the bus into 'Reg B.'

There is just one special situation in an ALU instruction, and that is when the operation is CMP, code 111. For a compare operation, we do not want to store any results back into 'Reg B.' Therefore, there is a three input AND gate connected to IR bits 1, 2 and 3, which is then connected to a NOT gate, and then to a third input on the AND gate that does step 6 of the ALU instruction. So when the operation is 111, the first AND will come on, the NOT will go off, and the output of the Step 6 AND gate will not turn on.

This ALU instruction is now done. Step 7 resets the stepper, which then goes through its steps again, fetching the next instruction, etc, etc.

We are going to invent one more thing here, and that is a shorthand way of writing CPU instructions on a piece of paper. In the Instruction Code, 1000 1011 means "Add R2 to R3," but it takes a lot of practice for a person to look at 1000 1011 and immediately think of addition and registers. It also would take a lot of memorization to think of it the other way around, that is, if you wanted to XOR two registers, what is the Instruction Code for XOR? It would be easier to write something like ADD R2,R3 or XOR R1,R1.

This idea of using a shorthand has a name, and it is called a computer language. So along with inventing an instruction code, we will also invent a computer language that represents the instruction code. The ALU instruction results in the first eight words of our new language.

Language	Meaning
ADD RA,RB	Add RA and RB and put answer in RB
SHR RA,RB	Shift RA Right and put answer in RB
SHL RA,RB	Shift RA Left and put the answer in RB
NOT RA,RB	Not RA and put the answer in RB
AND RA,RB	And RA and RB and put answer in RB
OR RA,RB	Or RA and RB and put answer in RB
XOR RA,RB	Exclusive OR RA and RB into RB
CMP RA,RB	Compare RA and RB

When a person wants to write a computer program, he can write it directly in the instruction code, or use a computer language. Of course, if you write a program in a computer language, it will have to be translated into the actual instruction code before it can be placed in RAM and executed.

The Load and Store Instructions

The Load and Store instructions are pretty simple. They move a byte between RAM and a register. They are very similar to each other so we will cover both of them in one chapter.

We'll get to the details of these instructions in a moment, but first we need to have something that tells us when we have a Load or Store instruction in the Instruction Register. With the ALU instruction, all we needed to know was that bit 0 was on. The code for every other type of instruction begins with bit 0 off, so if we connect a NOT gate to bit 0, when that NOT gate turns on, that tells us that we have some other type of instruction. In this computer, there are eight types of instructions that are not ALU instructions, so when bit 0 is off, we will use the next three bits of the IR to tell us exactly which type of instruction we have.

The three bits that went to the ALU in an ALU instruction also go to a 3x8 decoder here in the Control Section. As you remember, one and only one of the outputs of a decoder is on at all times, so we will have AND gates on the outputs to prevent any output from going anywhere during an ALU instruction. But when it is not an ALU instruction, the one output of the decoder that is on, will get through its AND gate, and in turn will be connected to some more gates that make the appropriate instruction work.

In the diagram below, you can see IR bits 1, 2 and 3 going into a decoder which has eight AND gates on its outputs. IR bit 0 has a NOT gate which goes to the other side of those eight AND gates. This decoder is used for the rest of the instructions that our computer will have.

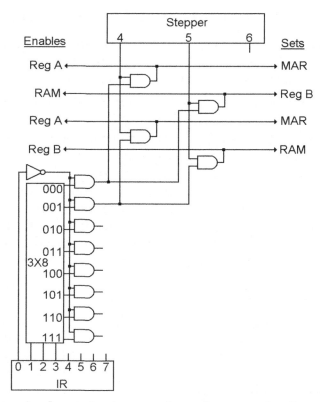

This chapter is about the instructions that use the first two outputs of the decoder, the ones that come on when the IR starts with 0000 or 0001.

The first instruction moves a byte from RAM to a register, this is called the "Load" instruction. The other one does the same in reverse, it moves a byte from a register to RAM, and is called the "Store" instruction.

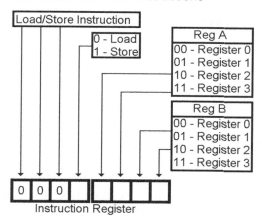

The Instruction Code for the Load instruction is 0000, and for the Store instruction is 0001. The remaining four bits in both cases specify two registers, just like the ALU instruction did, but in this case, one register will be used to select one of the locations in RAM, and the other register will either be loaded from, or stored to, that RAM location.

Step 4 is the same for both instructions. One of the registers is selected by IR bits 4 and 5 and is enabled onto bus. The bus is then set into MAR, thus selecting one address in RAM.

In step five, IR bits 6 and 7 select another one of the CPU registers. For the Load instruction, RAM is enabled onto the bus and the bus is set into the selected register. For the Store instruction, the selected register is enabled onto the bus and the bus is set into RAM.

Each of these instructions only need two steps to complete, step 6 will do nothing.

Here are two new words for our computer language:

Language		Meaning
LD	RA,RB	Load RB from RAM address in RA
ST	RA,RB	Store RB to RAM address in RA

The Data Instruction

Now here is an interesting instruction. All it does is load a byte from RAM into a Register like the Load instruction, above. The thing that is different about it though, is where in RAM it will get that byte.

In the Data instruction, the data comes from where the next instruction ought to be. So you could consider that this instruction is actually two bytes long! The first byte is the instruction, and the next byte is some data that will be placed into a register. This data is easy to find, because by the time we have the instruction in the IR, the IAR has already been updated, and so it points right to this byte.

Here is the Instruction Code for the Data instruction. Bits 0 to 3 are 0010. Bits 4 and 5 are not used. Bits 6 and 7 select the register that will be loaded with the data that is in the second byte.

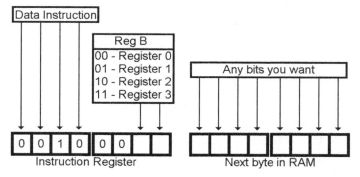

All this instruction needs to do is, in step 4, send IAR to MAR, and in step 5, send RAM to the desired CPU register. However, there is one more thing that needs to happen. Since the second byte of the instruction is just data that could be anything, we do not want to execute this second byte as an instruction. We need to add 1 to the IAR a second time so that it will skip this byte and point to the next instruction. We will do this the same way that it is done in steps 1 and 3. In step 4, when we send IAR to MAR, we will take advantage of the fact that the ALU is calculating IAR plus something at the same time, we will turn on the 'Bus 1,'

and set the answer into ACC. Step 5 still moves the data to a
Register, and in step 6 we can move ACC to IAR.

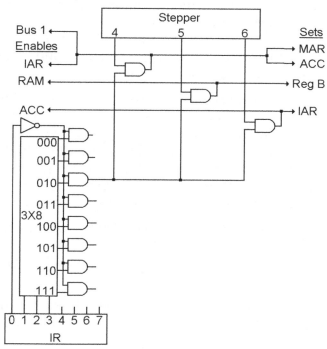

Here is another new word for our computer language:

Language	Meaning
DATA RB,xxxx xxxx	Load these 8 bits into RB

The Second Great Invention

The first great invention is this idea of having a string of instructions in RAM that get executed one by one by the CPU. But our clock is very fast, and the amount of RAM we have is limited. What will happen, in far less than a second, when we have executed every instruction in RAM?

Fortunately, we will not have to answer that question, because someone came up with another type of instruction that is so important that it qualifies as the second great invention necessary to allow the computer to do what it does. Because of the versatile arrangement of our CPU and its Control Section, it is an extremely simple thing to make this work, but its importance should not be lost because of this simplicity.

This new type of instruction is called a Jump instruction, and all it does is to change the contents of the IAR, thus changing where in RAM the next, and subsequent instructions will come from.

The exact type of Jump instruction described in this chapter is called a "Jump Register" instruction. It simply moves the contents of Reg B into the IAR. Here is the Instruction Code for it:

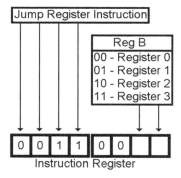

The computer is executing a series of instructions in RAM, one after the other, and suddenly one of those instructions changes the contents of the IAR. What will happen then? The next instruction that will be fetched will not be the one that follows the last one. It will be the one that is at whatever RAM address was loaded into the IAR. And it will carry on from that point with the next one, etc. until it executes another jump instruction.

The wiring for the Jump Register instruction only needs one step. In step 4, the selected register is enabled onto the bus, and set into the IAR, and that is all. If we wanted to speed up our CPU, we could use step 5 to reset the stepper. But to keep our diagram simple, we won't bother with that. Steps 5 an 6 will do nothing.

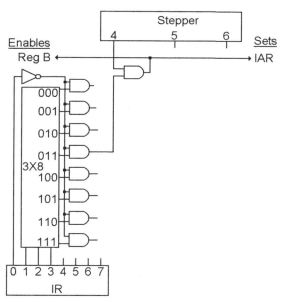

Here is another new word for our computer language:

Language	Meaning
JMPR RB	Jump to the address in RB

Another Way to Jump

This is another type of Jump instruction. It is similar to the Data instruction in that it uses two bytes. It replaces the IAR with the byte that is in RAM immediately following the instruction byte, thus changing where in RAM the next and subsequent instructions will come from. Here is the Instruction Code for it. Bits 4, 5, 6 and 7 are not used in this instruction:

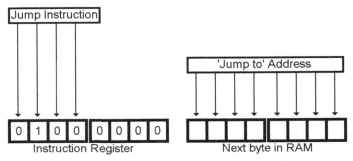

This exact type of Jump instruction is just called a "Jump." It is useful when you know the address that you are going to want to jump to, when you are writing the program. The Jump Register Instruction is more useful when the address you are going to want to jump to is calculated as the program in running, and may not always be the same.

One of the things you can do with a Jump instruction is to create a loop of instructions that execute over and over again. You can have a series of fifty instructions in RAM, and the last instruction "Jumps" back to the first one.

Like the Data instruction, the IAR already points to the byte we need. Unlike the Data Instruction, we don't need to add 1 to the IAR a second time because we are going to replace it anyway. So we only need two steps. In step 4, we send IAR to MAR. In step 5 we move the selected RAM byte to the IAR. Step 6 will do nothing.

Here is the wiring that makes it work:

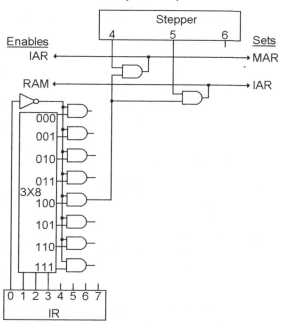

Here is another new word for our computer language:

Language   Meaning

JMP   Addr   Jump to the address in the next byte

The Third Great Invention

Here is the third, and last, invention that makes a computer a computer.

This is just like the Jump Instruction, but sometimes it jumps, and sometimes it doesn't. Of course, to jump or not to jump is just two possibilities, so it only takes one bit to determine which will happen. Mostly what we are going to introduce in this chapter is where that one bit comes from.

Do you remember the 'Carry' bit that comes out of, and goes back into the ALU? This bit comes either from the adder, or from one of the shifters. If you add two numbers that result in an amount that is greater than 255, the carry bit will come on. If you left shift a byte that has the left bit on, or right shift a byte that has the right bit on, these situations will also turn on the ALU's carry out bit.

There is also a bit that tells us if the two inputs to the ALU are equal, another one that tells us if the A input is larger, and one more bit that tells us if the output of the ALU is all zeros.

These bits are the only things that we have not yet found a home for in the CPU. These four bits will be called the "Flag" bits, and they will be used to make the decision for a "Jump If" instruction as to whether it will execute the next instruction in RAM or jump to some other address.

What we are trying to get the computer to be able to accomplish, is for it to first execute an ALU instruction, and then have one or more "Jump If" instructions following it. The "Jump If" will jump or not depending on something that happened during the ALU instruction.

Of course, by the time the "Jump If" is executing, the results of the ALU instruction are long gone. If you go back and look at the details of the ALU instruction, it is only during step 5 that all of the proper inputs are going into the ALU and the desired answer is coming out. It is at this time that the answer is set into ACC. The timing is the same for all four Flag bits, they are only valid during step 5 of the ALU instruction. Therefore, we need a way to save the state of the Flag bits as they were during step 5 of the ALU instruction.

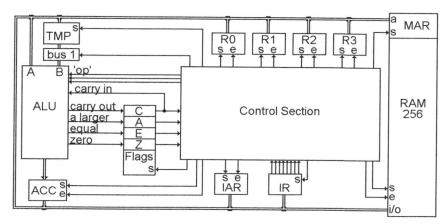

Here is the last register that we are going to add to the CPU. This will be called the FLAG register, and we are only going to use four bits of it, one for each of the flags.

The Flag bits from the ALU are connected to the input of this register, and it will be set during step 5 of the ALU instruction just like ACC and it will stay set that way until the next time an ALU instruction is executed. Thus if you have an ALU instruction followed by a "Jump If" instruction, the "Flag" bits can be used to "decide" whether to Jump or not.

Every instruction cycle uses the ALU in step 1 to add 1 to the address for the next instruction, but only step 5 of the ALU instruction has a connection that sets the Flags. (We did not show this connection in the wiring for the ALU instruction because we had not yet introduced the Flag Reg, but it will appear in the completed Control Section diagram.)

This combination of Flag bits, and the Jump IF instruction, is the third and last great invention that makes computers as we know them today, work.

Here is the Instruction Code for a 'Jump If' instruction. The second four bits of the instruction tell the CPU which flag or flags should be checked. You put a '1' in the instruction bit(s) corresponding to the flag(s) that you want to test for. If any one of the Flags that you test is on, the jump will happen. This arrangement gives us a number of ways to decide whether to jump or not. There is a second byte that contains the address to jump to, if the jump is taken.

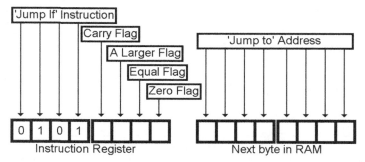

Here is the wiring in the Control Section that makes the Jump If instruction work.

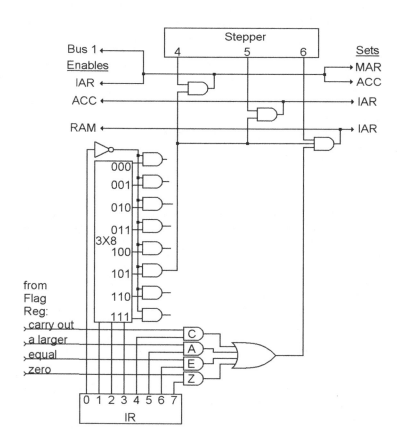

Step 4 moves IAR to MAR so we are prepared to get the 'Jump to Address' that we will use IF we jump. But because we might not jump, we also need to calculate the address of the next instruction in RAM. And so step 4 also turns on Bus 1 and sets the answer in ACC.

In step 5, we move ACC to IAR so we are ready to fetch the next instruction IF we don't jump.

Step 6 is where the "decision" is made. We will move the second byte of the instruction from RAM to IAR IF the third input to that AND gate is on. That third input comes from an OR gate with four inputs. Those four inputs come from the four Flag bits after being ANDed with the last four bits of the Jump If instruction in IR. If, for instance, there is a '1' in the 'Equal' bit of the instruction, and the 'Equal' Flag bit is on, then the jump will occur.

Here are more words for our computer language. 'J' means Jump, 'C' means Carry, 'A' means A is larger, 'E' means A Equals B and 'Z' means that the answer is all Zeros. Here are the words of the language that test a single Flag:

Language		Meaning
JC	Addr	Jump if Carry is on
JA	Addr	Jump if A is larger than B
JE	Addr	Jump if A is Equal to B
JZ	Addr	Jump if the answer is Zero

You can also test more than one flag bit at the same time by putting a 1 in more than one of the four bits. Actually since there are four bits, there are 16 possible combinations, but the one with all four bits off is not useful because it will never jump. For the sake of completeness, here are the rest of the possibilities:

Language		Meaning
JCA	Addr	Jump if Carry or A larger
JCE	Addr	Jump if Carry or A Equal B
JCZ	Addr	Jump if Carry or answer is Zero
JAE	Addr	Jump if A is larger or Equal to B
JAZ	Addr	Jump if A is larger or answer is Zero
JEZ	Addr	Jump if A Equals B or answer is Zero

JCAE Addr	Jump if Carry or A larger or Equal to B
JCAZ Addr	Jump if Carry or A larger or Zero
JCEZ Addr	Jump if Carry or A Equals B or Zero
JAEZ Addr	Jump if A larger or Equal to B or Zero
JCAEZ Addr	Jump if Carry, A larger, Equal or Zero

The Clear Flags Instruction

There is one annoying detail that we need to have here. When you do addition or shifting, you have the possibility of getting the carry flag turned on by the operation. This is necessary, we use it for the Jump If instruction as in the previous chapter.

The Carry Flag is also used as an input to the addition and shift operations. The purpose of this is so you can add numbers larger than 255 and shift bits from one register to another.

The problem that arises is that if you are just adding two single-byte numbers, you don't care about any previous Carry, but the Carry Flag may still be set from a previous operation. In that case, you might add 2+2 and get 5!

Bigger computers have several ways to do this, but for us, we will just have a Clear Flags Instruction that you need to use before any adds or shifts where an unexpected carry bit would be a problem.

Here is the Instruction Code for this instruction. Bits 4, 5, 6 and 7 are not used.

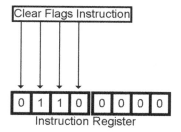

The wiring for this is very simple and a bit tricky. We will not enable anything onto the bus, thus it and the 'A' ALU input will be all zeros. We will turn on 'Bus 1' so the 'B' input is 0000 0001. We won't send an operation to the ALU, so it will be in ADD mode. The ALU, therefore, will be adding 0 and 1, and there may be a carry input. The answer then will be either 0000 0001 or 0000 0010. But there will be no carry output, the answer is not zero and B is larger than A so 'equal' and 'A larger' will both be off. We 'set' the Flag Reg at this time while all four Flag bits are off.

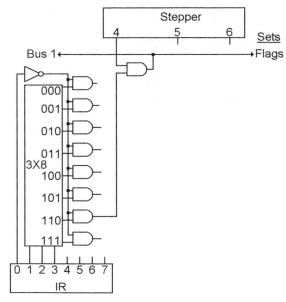

Here is another word for our language.

Language	Meaning
CLF	Clear all Flags

Ta Daa!

We have now wired up the Control Section of our CPU. As a result, we can place a series of instructions in RAM, and the Clock, Stepper, Instruction Register and wiring will fetch and execute those instructions. Here is the entire control section:

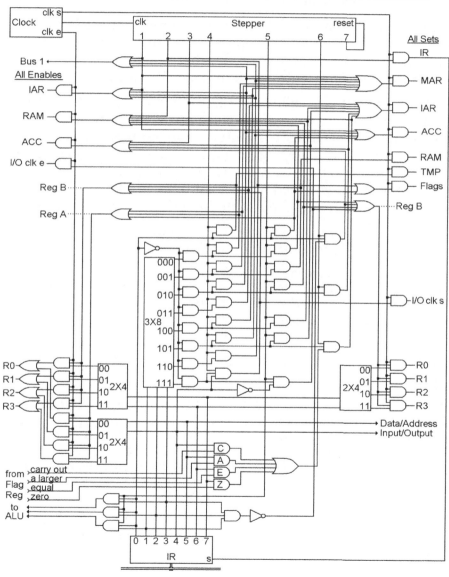

Yes, this looks pretty complicated, but we have looked at every part of it already. The only thing we had to add were some OR gates because most of the 'enables' and 'sets' need multiple connections. This actually has a lot fewer parts than the RAM, but that was much more repetitive. Most of the mess here is just getting the wires from one place to another.

The byte that is placed in the Instruction Register causes a certain activity to occur. Each possible pattern causes a different activity. Therefore, we have a code where each of the 256 possible codes represents a different specific activity.

As mentioned, this is called the Instruction Code. Another name for it is "machine language," because this is the only language (code) that the machine (computer) "understands." You "tell" the machine what to do by giving it a list of orders you want it to carry out. But you have to speak the only language that it "understands." If you feed it the right byte-sized patterns of ons and offs, you can make it do something that will be useful.

Here are all of the Instruction Codes and our shorthand language brought together in one place.

Instruction Code	Language		Meaning
1000 rarb	ADD	RA,RB	Add
1001 rarb	SHR	RA,RB	Shift Right
1010 rarb	SHL	RA,RB	Shift Left
1011 rarb	NOT	RA,RB	Not
1100 rarb	AND	RA,RB	And
1101 rarb	OR	RA,RB	Or
1110 rarb	XOR	RA,RB	Exclusive OR
1111 rarb	CMP	RA,RB	Compare
0000 rarb	LD	RA,RB	Load RB from RAM addr in RA
0001 rarb	ST	RA,RB	Store RB to RAM addr in RA
0010 00rb	DATA	RB,Addr	Load these 8 bits into RB
0011 00rb	JMPR	RB	Jump to the address in RB
0100 0000	JMP	Addr	Jump to the addr in the next byte
0101 caez	JCAEZ	Addr	Jump if any tested Flag is on
0110 0000	CLF		Clear all Flags

Believe it or not, everything you have ever seen a computer do, is simply the result of a CPU executing a long series of instructions such as the ones above.

A Few More Words on Arithmetic

We don't want to spend a lot of time on this subject, but the only thing that we have seen so far that looks like arithmetic is the adder, so we will look at simple examples of slightly more complex arithmetic. Not to teach you how to act like a computer, but just to prove to you that it works.

Here is how you do subtraction. It is done with the adder and the NOT gates. If you want to subtract R1 from R0, first you NOT R1 back into itself. Then you add 1 to R1, then you Add R0 to R1.

This shows an example of subtracting 21 from 37:

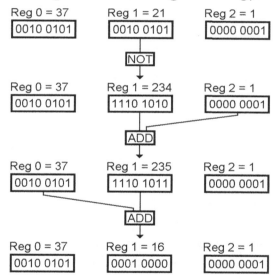

The last step is adding 37 + 235, the answer of which should be 272. But a single register cannot hold a number larger than 255. Therefore the adder turns on its Carry bit, and the eight bits remaining of the answer are 0001 0000, which is 16, the correct answer for 37 minus 21.

Why does NOTting and ADDing result in subtraction? Why do you have to add 1 after NOTting? Why do you ignore the carry bit? We are not going to attempt to answer any of these questions in this book. These are the details that keep a very few engineers from getting a good night's sleep. These brave people study these problems and design ways for ordinary people to not have to understand it.

Here is how you do multiplication. When we do multiplication with a pencil and paper in the decimal system, you have to remember your multiplication tables, you know, 3 times 8 equals 24, 6 times 9 equals 54, etc.

In binary, multiplication is actually much easier than in decimal. 1 times 1 equals 1, and for every other combination, the answer is 0! It just couldn't get much simpler than that! Here's an example of multiplying 5 times 5 with pencil and paper in binary.

```
              00000101
          x   00000101
              --------
              00000101
             00000000
            00000101
           00000000
          00000000
         00000000
        00000000
       00000000
       ----------------
       0000000000011001
```

If you look at what's happening here, if the right digit of the bottom number is a 1, you put the top number in the answer. Then, for every digit to the left of that, shift the top number left, and if the bottom digit is a 1, add the shifted top number to the answer. When you get through the eight bits of the bottom number, you're done.

So multiplication is accomplished with the adder and the shifters. It's as simple as that. You can write a simple program like this:

R0 contains the bottom number, R1 contains the top number and R2 will contain the answer. R3 is used to jump out of the loop after going through it eight times.

RAM Addr	Instruction	Comments
50	DATA R3,0000 0001	* Put '1' into R3
52	XOR R2,R2	* Put '0' in R2

53	CLF		* Clear Flags
54	SHR	R0	* One bit to Carry Flag
55	JC	59	* Do the ADD
57	JMP	61	* Skip the ADD
59	CLF		* Clear Flags
60	ADD	R1,R2	* ADD this line
61	CLF		* Clear Flags
62	SHL	R1	* Mult top by 2
63	SHL	R3	* Shift counter
64	JC	68	* Out if done
66	JMP	53	* Do next step
68	(Next instruction in program)		

See what happens with the Registers as this program goes through its loop the first three times.

R0	R1	R2	R3

At start (after 52):

0000 0101   0000 0101   0000 0000   0000 0001

First time (after 63):

0000 0010   0000 1010   0000 0101   0000 0010

Second time (after 63):

0000 0001   0001 0100   0000 0101   0000 0100

Third time (after 63):

0000 0000   0010 1000   0001 1001   0000 1000

The important thing that has happened here is that R1 has been added to R2 twice. It happened on the first time through, when R1 contained 0000 0101, and on the third time through, after R1 had been shifted left twice and therefore contained 0001 0100. R2 now contains 0001 1001 binary, which is 16+8+1, or 25 decimal, which is the correct answer for 5 times 5. The loop will repeat 5 more times until the bit in R3 gets shifted out to the Carry Flag, but the total won't increase because there are no more 1s in R0.

This program will go through eight times. We start with 0000 0001 in R3. Near the end of the program, R3 gets shifted left.

The first seven times through, there will be no carry, so the program will get to the 'JMP 53' and go back up to the third instruction of the program. The eighth time R3 gets shifted left, the one bit that is on gets shifted out of R3 and into the Carry flag. Therefore, the 'JC 68' will jump over the 'JMP 53' and carry on with whatever instructions come after this.

The byte in R0 gets shifted right to test which bits are on. The byte in R1 gets shifted left to multiply it by two. When there was a bit in R0, you add R1 to R2. And that's all there is to it.

One thing we do not address in this example is what happens if the answer of the multiplication is more than 255. If a multiplication program multiplies two one-byte numbers, it ought to be able to handle a two-byte answer. That would take care of any two numbers that you might start with. This would be accomplished with the carry flag and some more Jump If instructions. We won't torture the reader with the details.

Reading a program like the one above is an entirely different skill than reading the diagrams and graphs we have seen so far in the book. I hope you were able to follow it, but no one is expected to become an expert at reading programs because of this book.

Division also can be done by our computer. There are several ways it can be done, and we are not going to examine any of them in any detail. Just imagine the following simple method. Lets say you want to divide fifteen by three. If you repeatedly subtract three from fifteen, and count the number of subtractions you can accomplish before the fifteen is all gone, that count will be the answer. Like these five steps: (1)15-3=12, (2)12-3=9, (3)9-3=6, (4)6-3-3, (5)3-3=0. This is easily turned into a program.

Computers also have ways of handling negative numbers and numbers with decimal points. The details are very tedious, and studying them would not enhance our understanding of how computers work. It still comes down to nothing more than

NAND gates. Our simple computer could do all of these things with programs.

The Outside World

What we have described so far is the whole computer. It has two parts, the RAM and the CPU. That's all there is. These simple operations are the most complicated things that a computer can do. The ability to execute instructions, modify bytes with the ALU, the ability to jump from one part of the program to another, and most importantly, the ability to jump or not jump based on the result of a calculation. This is what a computer is able to do. These are simple things, but since it operates so quickly, it can do huge numbers of these operations that can result in something that looks impressive.

These two parts make it a computer, but if all the computer could do is run a program and rearrange bytes in RAM, no one would ever know what it was doing. So there is one more thing that the computer needs in order to be useful, and that is a way to communicate with the outside world.

Dealing with anything outside of the computer is called 'Input/Output' or 'I/O' for short. Output means data going out of the computer; Input means data coming into the computer. Some things are input only, such as a keyboard, some things are output only, like a display screen, some things do both input and output, like a disk.

All we need for I/O is a few wires, and a new instruction.

For the wires, all we are going to do is to extend the CPU bus outside of the computer and add four more wires to go with it. This combination of 12 wires will be called the I/O Bus. Everything that is connected to the computer is attached to this one I/O bus.

The devices that are connected to the I/O bus are called 'peripherals,' because they are not inside the computer, they are outside of the computer, on its periphery (the area around it.)

More than one thing can be attached to the I/O bus, but the computer controls the process, and only one of these things is active at a time.

Each thing attached to the I/O bus has to have its own unique I/O address. This is not the same as the addresses of the bytes in RAM, it is just some 'number' that the peripheral will recognize when placed on the bus.

Here is what the I/O bus looks like in the CPU, there at the bottom right of the drawing.

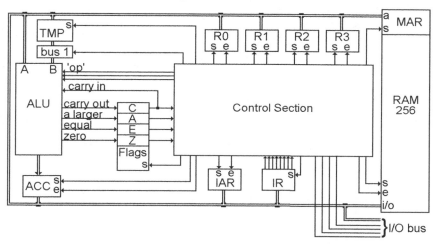

In the diagram below are the wires of the I/O Bus. The CPU Bus is the same eight-wire bundle that goes everywhere else. The 'Input/Output' wire determines which direction data will be moving on the CPU bus, either in or out. The 'Data/Address' wire tells us whether we will be transferring a byte of data, or an I/O Address that selects one of the many devices that could be attached to the I/O bus. 'I/O Clk e' and 'I/O Clk s' are used to enable and set registers so that bytes can be moved back and forth.

```
     CPU Bus  ═══════════════════════
 Input/Output  ───────────────────────
 Data/Address  ───────────────────────
    I/O clk e  ───────────────────────
    I/O clk s  ───────────────────────
```

Here is the control section wiring for the new instruction that controls the I/O bus. This shows where the four new wires for the I/O bus come from. They are at the bottom right of the drawing. They were also shown on the full control section diagram a few chapters back. Sorry if that was confusing, but having that diagram in the book once was enough.

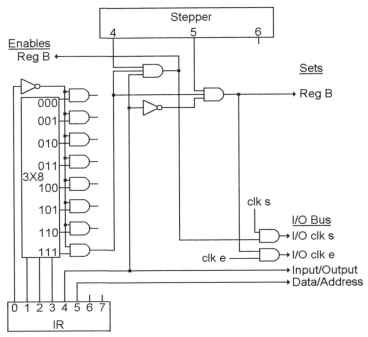

IR bits 4 and 5 are placed on the I/O bus at all times. To make the I/O operation happen, only one step is needed. For Output, Reg B is enabled, and I/O Clk s is turned on and off during step 4. Steps 5 and 6 do nothing. For Input, I/O Clk e is enabled, and Reg B is set during step 5. Steps 4 and 6 do nothing.

Here is the Instruction Code for the I/O instruction:

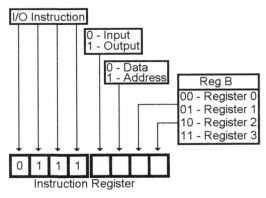

This one instruction can be used in four different ways depending on IR bits 4 and 5, and therefore there are four new words for our language.

Language		Meaning
IN	Data,RB	Input I/O Data to RB
IN	Addr,RB	Input I/O Address to RB
OUT	Data,RB	Output RB to I/O as Data
OUT	Addr,RB	Output RB to I/O as Address

Each I/O device has its own unique characteristics, and therefore needs unique parts and wiring to connect it to the I/O bus. The collection of parts that connects the device to the bus is called a "device adapter." Each type of adapter has a specific name such as the 'keyboard adapter' or the 'disk adapter.'

The adapter does nothing unless its address appears on the bus. When it does, then the adapter will respond to the commands that the computer sends to it.

With an 'OUT Addr' instruction, the computer turns on the address wire, and puts the address of the device it wants to talk to, on the CPU bus. The peripheral recognizes its address and comes to life. Every other peripheral has some other address, so they won't respond.

We are not going to describe every gate in the I/O system. By this time, you should believe that bytes of information can be transferred over a bus with a few control wires. The message of this chapter is only the simplicity of the I/O system. The CPU and the RAM are the computer. Everything else, disks, printers, keyboards, the mouse, the display screen, the things that make sound, the things that connect to the internet, all these things are peripherals, and all they are capable of doing is accepting bytes of data from the computer or sending bytes of data to the computer. The adapters for different devices have different capabilities, different numbers of registers, and different requirements as far as what the program running in the CPU must do to operate the device properly. But they don't do anything fancier than that. The computer controls the process with a very few simple I/O commands that are executed by the CPU.

The Keyboard

A keyboard is one of the simplest peripherals connected to the I/O bus. It is an input only device, and just presents one byte at a time to the CPU.

The keyboard has eight wires inside, its own little bus as shown on the right. When you press a key, it simply connects electricity to the wires necessary to create the ASCII code corresponding to the key that was pressed. That little box that says 'Control,' is also notified when a key is pressed, and sets the ASCII code into the Keycode Register.

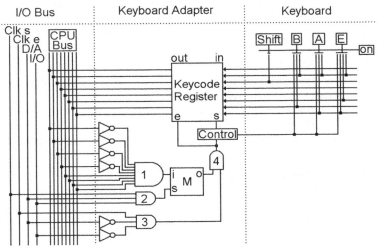

After pressing a key, there will be an ASCII code waiting in the Keycode Register. Here's how the CPU gets that code into one of its registers.

AND gate #1 has eight inputs. They are connected to the CPU bus, four of them through NOT gates. Thus this AND gate will turn on any time the bus contains 0000 1111. This is the I/O address of this keyboard adapter.

AND gate #2 comes on only during 'clk s' time of an OUT Addr instruction. It operates the 'set' input of a Memory bit. If the bus contains 0000 1111 at this time, the 'i' input will be on, and the Memory bit will turn on. When this Memory bit is on, it means that the keyboard adapter is active.

AND gate #3 comes on during 'clk e' time of an IN Data instruction. If the Memory bit is on, AND gate #4 will come on and the Keycode Register will be enabled onto the bus, which will be set into Reg B in the CPU.

Every adapter that is connected to the I/O bus needs to have the type of circuitry we see in gates #1 and #2 and the memory bit above. Each adapter will have a different combination that turns gate #1 on; this is what allows the CPU to select each adapter individually.

Here is a little program that moves the current keypress into Reg 3 in the CPU.

Instruction		Comments
Data	R2,0000 1111	* Put Addr of Keyboard in Reg 2
OUT	Addr,R2	* Select Keyboard
IN	Data,R3	* Get ASCII of key pressed
XOR	R2,R2	* Clear Address in Reg 2
OUT	Addr,R2	* Un-Select Keyboard

That little 'Control' box clears the Keycode Register after it has been sent to the CPU.

The program running in the CPU will check the keyboard adapter on a regular basis, and if the byte that it receives is all zeros, then no key has been pressed. If the byte has one or more bits on, then the program will do whatever the program has been designed to do with a keystroke at that time.

Again, we are not going to go through every gate in the Keyboard adapter. All device adapters have the same sorts of circuitry in order to be able to respond when they are addressed, and send or receive bytes of information as needed. But it is no more complicated than that. That is all that I/O devices and adapters do.

The Display Screen

Television and computer display screens work the same way, the main difference between them is only what they display. This is not actually computer technology, because you don't need a display screen to have a computer, but most computers do have a screen, and the computer spends a lot of its time making the screen look like something, so we need to know a little bit about how it works.

Television appears to give you moving pictures with sound. The pictures and sound are done separately, and in this chapter, we are only concerned with how the picture works.

The first thing to know is that although the picture appears to be moving, it is actually a series of still pictures presented so quickly that the eye doesn't notice it. You probably already knew that, but here's the next thing. You have seen motion picture film. It is a series of pictures. To watch a movie, you put the film in a projector, which shines light through one picture, then moves the film to the next picture, shines light through it, etc. It usually runs at 24 pictures per second, which is fast enough to give the illusion of a constantly moving picture.

Television goes a bit faster, about 30 pictures per second, but there is another, much bigger difference between film and television. With the movie film, each still picture is shown all at once. Each picture is complete, when you shine the light through it, every part of the picture appears on the screen simultaneously. Television is not capable of doing this. It does not have a whole picture to put on the screen all at once.

All that a television can do at one instant in time, is to light up one single dot on the screen. It lights up one dot, then another dot, then another, very quickly until one whole picture's worth of dots has been lit. This whole screen's worth of dots makes up one still picture, thus it has to light up all of the dots within one thirtieth of a second, and then do it all over again with the next picture, etc. until it has placed 30 picture's worth of dots on the screen in one second. So the TV is very busy lighting up individual dots, 30 times the number of dots on the screen, every second.

Usually, the top left dot is lit first, then the one to its right, and so on across the top of the screen to the top right corner. Then it starts with the second line of dots, going across the screen again, the third line, etc. until it has scanned the entire screen. The brightness of each dot is high or low so that each part on the screen gets lit up to the proper brightness to make the screen look like the intended image.

At any one instant in time, the television is only dealing with one single solitary dot on the screen. So with television, there are two illusions – the illusion of motion coming from a series of still pictures, as well as the illusion of complete still pictures that are actually drawn one dot at a time. This second illusion is aided by what the screen in made of, each dot only gets lit up for a tiny fraction of a second, and it starts to fade away immediately. Fortunately, whatever the screen is made of that glows, continues to glow to some degree between one time when the dot is lit up and 1/30th of a second later when that same dot gets lit up again.

To the eye, you just see a moving picture, but there are a lot of things going on to make it appear that way.

In a computer, a single dot on the screen is called a 'picture element,' or 'pixel' for short.

Computer screens work just like televisions. They also have to scan the entire screen 30 times a second to light up each individual pixel and thereby make an image appear. Even if the content of the screen is not changing, something in the computer has to scan that unchanging image onto the screen 30 times every second. No scanning, no picture – that's just the way it works.

We're not going to go into the same amount of detail here that we did with the CPU and the RAM, those two are what make it a computer, but if we want to know how our computer is able to put something on the screen that we can read, we need to have the basic idea of how it works.

In this chapter we will look at the simplest kind of screen, the kind that is black and white, and whose pixels can only either be fully on or fully off. This type of screen can display characters and the type of pictures that are made of line drawings. Later in the book we will see the few simple changes that enable a screen to display things like color photographs.

The major parts are three. First there is the computer, we have seen how that works. It has an I/O Bus that can move bytes to and from things outside of the computer. Second is the screen. The screen is just a large grid of pixels, each of which can be selected, one at a time, and while selected, can either be turned on, or not. The third item is the 'display adapter.' The display adapter is connected to the I/O Bus on one side, and to the screen on the other side.

The heart of a display adapter is some RAM. The display adapter needs its own RAM so it can "remember" which pixels should be on, and which pixels should be off. In the type of screen we are going to describe here, there needs to be one bit in RAM for each pixel on the screen.

In order to make the screen scan every pixel 30 times every second, the Display Adapter needs its own clock that ticks at a speed that is 30 times the number of pixels on the screen. At each tick of the clock, one pixel is selected and it is turned on or not by the corresponding bit from the RAM.

As an example, lets use an old type of screen. It is a black and white screen that displays 320 pixels across the screen and 200 pixels down. That comes out to 64,000 individual pixels on the screen. Each pixel on the screen has a unique address consisting of two numbers, the first being the left-right or horizontal position, and the other being the up-down or vertical position. The address of the top left pixel is 0,0 and the bottom right pixel is 319,199

64,000 pixels times 30 pictures per second means that this Display Adapter's clock needs to tick 1,920,000 times per second. And since there are eight bits in a byte, we will need 8,000 bytes of display RAM to tell each of the 64,000 screen pixels whether to be on or off.

The display adapter has a register that sets the horizontal position of the current pixel. The display adapter adds 1 to this register at every tick of the clock. It starts at zero, and when the number in it gets to 319, the next step resets it back to zero. So it goes from zero to 319 over and over again. There is also a register that sets the vertical position of the current pixel. Every time the horizontal register gets reset to zero, the display adapter adds 1 to the vertical register. When the vertical register reaches 199, the next step will reset it to zero. So as the horizontal register goes from zero to 319 200 times, the vertical register goes from zero to 199 once.

The currently selected screen pixel is controlled by these registers, so as the horizontal register goes from 0 to 319, the current pixel goes across the screen once. Then the vertical register has one added to it, and the current pixel moves down to the first pixel on the next line.

Thus, the clock and the horizontal and vertical registers select each pixel on the screen, one at a time, going left to right in one row, then selecting each pixel in the next row down, then the next, etc. until every pixel on the screen has been selected one time. Then it starts all over again.

At the same time, there is another register that contains a display RAM address. This register also gets stepped through, although we only need one new byte for every eight pixels. The bits of each byte, one at a time, are sent to the screen at eight consecutive pixels to turn them on or off. After every eight pixels, the RAM address register has 1 added to it. By the time all of the pixels have been stepped through, the entire RAM has also been stepped through, and one entire picture has been drawn. When the horizontal and vertical registers have both reached their maximums, and are reset to zero, the RAM address is also reset to zero.

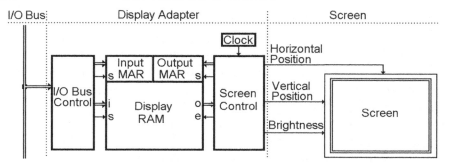

The display adapter spends most of its time painting the screen. The only other thing it has to do is to accept commands from the I/O Bus that will change the contents of the display adapter RAM. When the program running in the CPU needs to change what's on the screen, it will use the I/O OUT command to select the display adapter, and then send a display adapter RAM address and then a byte of data to store at that address. Then as the adapter continues to repaint the screen, the new data will appear on the screen at the appropriate spot.

The display adapter RAM is built differently than the RAM in our computer. It keeps the input and output functions separate. The inputs of all storage locations are connected to the input bus, and the outputs of all storage locations are connected to the output bus, but the input bus and the output bus are kept separate. Then there are two separate memory address registers, one for input and one for output. The input MAR has a grid that only selects which byte will be 'set,' and the output MAR has a separate grid that only selects which byte will be 'enabled.'

With this setup, the screen and the display RAM can both be continuously scanned using only the output MAR and the enable bit. When the I/O Bus is used to write into the display RAM, it uses only the input MAR and the set bit.

This is how the display adapter creates an image on the screen. Because of the way it works, there is an interesting relationship between which bits in the display RAM correspond to which pixels on the screen. As it scans the first eight pixels of the top line, it uses the individual bits of byte 0 of its RAM to turn the pixels on or off. As it scans the second eight pixels, it uses the individual bits of byte 1 of its RAM, etc. It takes 40 bytes of RAM to draw the first line, and so the last eight pixels, which are numbered 312 through 319, come from RAM byte 39. The second row uses byte 40 to draw its first 8 pixels, etc.

If you want to write letters and numbers on the screen, how do you do it? If you put the ASCII code for 'A' into a byte in the display RAM, you will just get eight pixels in a row where one is off, then one is on, then five are off and the last one is on. That's not what an 'A' should look like.

There is a solution for this, and it involves...

Another Code

When you want to print or display written language, you need to translate the ASCII code into something that is readable by a live person. We have a code, 0100 0101, that appears on the ASCII code table next to the letter 'E.' But how does the computer turn 0100 0101 into a readable 'E'?

We have a display screen, but the screen is a just a grid of pixels, there are no human readable 'E's in anything we have described so far. In order to get an 'E' on the screen, there has to be something that makes that shape that we recognize as a letter of the alphabet.

Therefore, we need another code. This code is really about little pictures made out of dots. For each character that we want to be able to draw on the screen, we need a little picture of that character. If you take a grid 8 pixels wide and 8 pixels high, you could decide which pixels had to be on to make a little picture that looks like the character that you want to draw on the screen, like this:

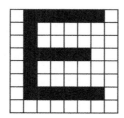

If you turn this picture into ons and offs, you could store it in eight bytes. If there are 100 different characters that you want to be able to display on the screen, then you'd need 100 different little pictures like this, and it would require 800 bytes of RAM to store it. Our little computer only has a 256 byte RAM, so this would be a good time to imagine that larger version that we described earlier.

These 800 bytes are a type of code known as a "font."

If you want to make a character appear in a certain place on the screen, you need to choose the correct little picture from the font, and then use I/O instructions to copy the eight bytes of the picture to the proper bytes in the display adapter's RAM.

If the pictures in our font are arranged in the same order as the ASCII code table, then we can use the numeric value of an ASCII code to find the corresponding picture within the font. The ASCII code for 'E' is 0100 0101. If you apply the binary number code to the same pattern of ones and zeros, you get the decimal number 69. 'E' then, is the 69th code in ASCII, and the picture of an 'E' will be the 69th picture within the font. Since there are eight bytes in each picture, you multiply the 69 by 8, and that tells you that the picture for 'E' will be the eight bytes starting at address 552.

Now we need to know where to copy these bytes to in the display RAM. Lets say that we want to display an 'E' at the very top left of the screen. Where are the bits that turn on the pixels that we are interested in? Well, the first line is easy, it is the first eight bits of the display RAM, Address 0. So we use a series of OUT instructions to copy RAM address 552 to display RAM address 0. Now, where is the second line in the display RAM? The display paints all 320 bits of the top row before it moves down to the second row. That means that it uses 40 bytes on each row, so the top row uses bytes 0-39. That means that the second byte of the picture of 'E' at RAM address 553 needs to be written at address 40 in the display RAM. Similarly, the third through eighth bytes get written at bytes 80, 120, 160, 200, 240 and 280. When you have done all of that, you would then see a complete 'E' on the screen. If you wanted to write an 'X' on the screen right next to the 'E', you would locate the eight bytes in the font for 'X' and copy them into display RAM bytes 1, 41, 81, 121, 161, 201, 241 and 281. If you need 27 'E's on your screen, you just copy the one 'E' in your font to 27 different places in the display RAM.

RAM Address	Byte Contents	Display RAM Address	Screen Pixels	Screen
552	01111110	000		E
553	01000000	040		
554	01000000	080		
555	01111100	120		
556	01000000	160		
557	01000000	200		
558	01111110	240		
559	00000000	280		

Of course, this seems like a lot of work just to make a single letter appear on the screen. The program that does this would need a loop of instructions that calculates the first 'from' and 'to' addresses, then issues the appropriate OUT instructions to copy the first byte to the display RAM. Then the loop would repeat, updating both addresses each time, until all eight bytes had been copied to the appropriate places. We're not going to write this program, but it could easily be a 50 instruction program that has to loop around eight times before it's finished. That means that it could take 400 instruction cycles just to put one character on the screen! If you drew 1000 characters on the screen, that might take 400,000 instruction cycles. On the other hand, that's still only about one quarter of one percent of what this computer can do in one second.

This just goes to show you why computers need to be so fast. The individual things that they do are so small, that it takes a huge number of steps to get anything done at all.

The Final Word on Codes

We have seen several codes used in our computer. Each one was designed for a specific purpose. Individual coded messages are put in bytes, and moved around and used to get things done.

The bytes do not 'know' which code was used to choose the pattern that they contain. There is nothing in the byte itself that tells you which code it is supposed to be.

Certain parts of the computer are built with various codes in mind. In the ALU, the adder and comparator are built to treat bytes as though they contain values encoded with the binary number code. So are the Memory Address Register and the Instruction Address Register.

The Instruction Register is built to treat its contents as though it contains values encoded with the Instruction Code.

The Display adapter RAM bits are just ons or offs for individual pixels. Pictures and fonts are strings of bytes that will result in something that can be recognized by a person when it is organized, and the brightnesses are set, by the wiring of a display adapter and screen.

The ASCII code table does not appear anywhere inside the computer because there is no way to represent a letter of the alphabet except by using a code.

The only places where ASCII gets converted between characters and the code for the character, are in the peripherals. When you press 'E' on the keyboard, you get the ASCII code for an 'E.' When you send the ASCII code for an 'E' to a printer, it prints the letter 'E.' The people who build these peripherals have an ASCII code table in front of them, and when they build a keyboard, the switch under the fourth button in the second row, which has the letter 'E' printed on it, is wired up to the proper bus wires to produce the code that appears next to the letter 'E' on the ASCII code table.

An 'E' is the fifth letter of an alphabet used by people to represent sounds and words in the process of writing down their spoken language. The only 'E's in the computer are the one on the keyboard and the ones that appear on the screen. All the 'E's that are in bytes are just the code that appears next to the 'E' on an ASCII code table. They are not 'E's, there is no way to put an 'E' in a computer. Even if you put a picture of an 'E' in a computer, it isn't actually an 'E' until it is displayed on the screen. That's when a person can look at it and say "That's an E."

Bytes are dumb. They just contain patterns of ons and offs. If a byte contains 0100 0101, and you send it to the printer, it will print the letter 'E.' If you send it to the Instruction Register, the computer will execute a Jump instruction. If you send it to the Memory Address Register, it will select byte number 69 of the RAM. If you send it to one side of the Adder, it will add 69 to whatever is on the other side of the Adder. If you send it to the display screen, it will set three pixels on and five pixels off.

Each of these pieces of the computer is designed with a code in mind, but once it is built, the mind is gone and even the code is gone. It just does what it was designed to do.

There is no limit to the codes that can be invented and used in a computer. Programmers invent new codes all the time. Like the cash register in the fast food restaurant mentioned earlier, somewhere in that machine is a bit that means 'include French fries.'

The Disk

Most computers have a disk. This is simply another peripheral that is attached to the I/O bus. The disk's mission is very simple; it can do two things. You can send it bytes, which it will store, or you can tell it to send back some bytes, which were stored previously.

There are two reasons that most computers have a disk. First, they have the ability to store a huge number of bytes, many times greater than the Computer's RAM. The CPU can only execute programs that are in RAM, it can only manipulate bytes that are in RAM. But there is never enough RAM to store all of the things that you may want to do with your computer. And so a disk will hold everything, and when you want to do one thing, the bytes on the disk for that one thing will be copied into RAM and used. Then when you want to do something different, the bytes for the new activity will be copied from the disk into the same area of RAM that had been used for the first activity.

The second reason that computers have disks, is that the bytes stored on the disk do not disappear when you turn the power off. The RAM loses its settings when you turn the computer off, when you turn it back on, all bytes are 0000 0000, but the disk retains everything that has been written on it.

A computer bit has been defined so far as a place where there is or is not some electricity. But prior to that, we defined it as a place that can be in one of two different states. On a disk, the electric bits are transformed into places on the surface of the disk that have been magnetized one way or the other. Since magnets have north and south poles, the spot on the disk can be magnetized either north-south or south-north. One direction would represent a zero, and the other direction, a one. Once a spot is magnetized, it stays that way unless the same spot gets magnetized the other way. Turning the power off has no effect on the magnetized spots.

A disk, as its name implies, is a round thing, that spins around quickly. It is coated with a material that can be magnetized easily. Do you remember the telegraph? At the receiving end, there is a piece of metal with a wire wrapped around it. That piece of metal turns into a magnet when electricity moves through the wire. The disk has a tiny version of this called a 'head' mounted on an arm. The arm holds the head very close to the surface of the spinning disk, and the arm can swing back and forth, so that the head can reach any point on the surface of the disk. If you put electricity through the head, it can magnetize the surface of the disk. Also, it works the other way around; when the head passes over a magnetized area, it makes electricity appear in the wires wrapped around the head. Thus, the head can either write on the disk or read what has been previously written on the disk. The bits of the bytes are written one after another on the disk surface.

The surface of the disk is divided into a series of rings, called tracks, very close to each other. The head can move across the surface and stop on any one of the tracks. Each circular track is usually divided into short pieces called sectors. Since a disk has two sides, usually both sides are coated with the magnetic material and there is a head on each side.

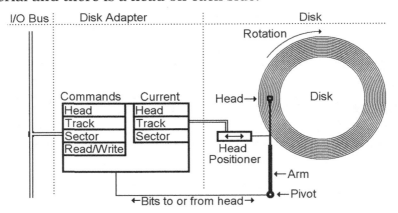

In RAM, every byte has its own address. On a disk, there is also a way to locate bytes, but it is very different. You have to specify which head, which track and which sector at which a block of bytes is located. That is the type of "address" that the data on a disk has, like "Head 0, Track 57, Sector 15." And at that address, there is not just one byte, but a block of bytes, typically several thousand. For the examples in our book, since our RAM is so small, we will talk about a disk that stores blocks of 100 bytes.

When a disk is read or written, there is no way to access an individual byte in the block of bytes. The whole block has to be transferred to RAM, worked on in RAM, and then the whole block has to be written back to the disk.

The disk spins quickly, faster than that fan on your desk; many popular disks spin 7200 times a minute, which is 120 times per second. That's pretty fast, but compared to the CPU, it is still pretty slow. In the time that the disk spins around one time, the Clock will tick over eight million times, and our CPU will execute well over a million instructions.

The disk, like every peripheral, is connected to its own adapter, which in turn is connected to the I/O bus. The disk adapter does a few things. It accepts commands to select a head, select a track and select a sector. It accepts commands to read from or write to, the block of bytes at the currently selected head, track and sector. There will also probably be a command where the CPU can check the current position of the arm and the disk.

The command to select a head can be completed immediately, but when it gets a command to select a track, it has to move the head to that track, which takes a long time in terms of instruction cycles. When it gets a command to select a sector, it has to wait for that sector to spin around to where the head is, which also takes a long time in terms of instruction cycles. When the CPU has determined that the head has arrived at the desired track and sector, then the I/O commands for reading or writing can be executed, and one byte at a time will be transferred over the I/O bus. A program that reads or writes a block of bytes has to continue the process until the whole block of bytes is complete. With our simple I/O system, the individual bytes move between the disk and a CPU register. The program that is running has to move these bytes to or from RAM, usually in consecutive locations.

This is all that a disk does. You have probably used a computer that had a disk, and didn't need to know anything about heads, tracks and sectors. And that is a good thing, because it is pretty annoying to have to deal with a disk at that level of detail. We will look at how a disk is normally used later in the book.

Another language note: There are several words that mean virtually the same thing, but for some reason certain words go with certain technologies.

If you want to send someone a letter, first you write it on a piece of paper, then when the recipient gets the letter, he reads it.

In the days of tape recorders, you would start with a blank tape. Then you would record some music on the tape. When you wanted to hear the music again you would play the tape.

When it comes to computer disks, putting something on the disk is called writing. Getting something off the disk is called reading.

Putting something into RAM is called writing or storing. Getting something out of RAM is called reading or retrieving.

Putting something into a CPU register is usually called loading.

Putting music on a disk is sometimes called recording, sometimes burning. Listening to a disk is still usually called playing, but if you are copying it onto your computer, then it is called ripping.

Writing, recording, storing, loading and burning all mean pretty much the same thing. Reading, retrieving, playing and ripping are also very similar. They mean the same things, it's just a difference of words.

Excuse Me Ma'am

There is one other thing that most computers have as part of their Input/Output system. A computer doesn't need one of these to be called a computer, so we will not go through every gate needed to build it. But it is a very common thing, so we will describe how it works.

You know if Mom is in the kitchen stirring a pot of soup, and little Joey comes running in and says "I want a glass of milk," Mom will put down the spoon, go over to the cabinet, get a glass, go to the refrigerator, pour the milk, hand it to Joey, and then she will go back to the stove, pick up the spoon and resume stirring the soup. The soup stirring was interrupted by getting a glass of milk, and then the soup stirring resumed.

This thing that most computers have, is called an "Interrupt," and it works very much like what happened with Mom and Joey.

An interrupt starts with one more wire added to the I/O Bus. This wire is used by certain device adapters to let the CPU know that it's a good time for the CPU to do an I/O operation, like right after someone presses a key on the keyboard. When a device adapter turns the Interrupt bit on, the next time the stepper gets back to step 1, the next instruction cycle will not do the usual fetch and execute, but rather it will do of the following:

Step 1	move binary 0 to MAR
Step 2	move IAR to RAM
Step 3	move binary 1 to MAR
Step 4	move Flags to RAM
Step 5	move binary 2 to MAR
Step 6	move RAM to IAR
Step 7	move binary 3 to MAR
Step 8	move RAM to Flags

The result of this sequence is that the current IAR and Flags are saved to RAM addresses 0 and 1, and they are replaced with the contents of RAM bytes addresses 2 and 3. Then the CPU returns to its normal fetch and execute operation. But the IAR has been replaced! So the next instruction will be fetched from whatever address was in RAM byte 2.

In other words, what the CPU had been doing is saved, and the CPU is sent off to do something else. If at the end of this new activity, the program puts RAM bytes 0 and 1 back into the IAR and Flags, the CPU will pick up from exactly where it left off, before it was interrupted.

This system is very useful for dealing with I/O operations. Without interrupts, the program running in the CPU would have to make sure to check all of the devices on the I/O Bus on a regular basis. With interrupts, the program can just do whatever it is designed to do, and the program that deals with things like keyboard input will be called automatically as needed by the interrupt system.

We have not included this in our CPU because it would just make our Control Section wiring diagram too big. It would need to add the following: two more steps to the stepper, wiring to do the above 8 steps in place of the normal instruction cycle, paths for the Flags register to get to and from the bus, a method of sending a binary 0, 1, 2 or 3 to MAR, and an instruction that restores RAM bytes 0 and 1 to the IAR and Flags register.

And that is an Interrupt system. As far as the language is concerned, the computer designers took an existing verb, 'interrupt,' and used it in three ways: It is a verb in "the keyboard interrupted the program," it is an adjective in "This is the Interrupt system," and it is a noun in "the CPU executed an interrupt."

That's All Folks

Yes, this is the end of our description of a computer. This is all there is. Everything you see a computer do is a long concatenation of these very simple operations, the ADDing, NOTting, Shifting, ANDing, ORing, XORing of bytes, Storing, Loading, Jumping and I/O operations, via the execution of the instruction code from RAM. This is what makes a computer a computer. This is the sum total of the smarts in a computer. This is all the thinking that a computer is capable of. It is a machine that does exactly what it is designed to do, and nothing more. Like a hammer, it is a tool devised by man to do tasks defined by man. It does its task exactly as designed. Also like a hammer, if it is thrown indiscriminately it can do something unpredictable and destructive.

The variety of things the computer can be made do is limited only by the imagination and cleverness of the people who create the programs for them to run. The people who build the computers keep making them faster, smaller, cheaper and more reliable.

When we think of a computer, we probably think of that box that sits on a desk and has a keyboard, mouse, screen and printer attached to it. But computers are used in many places. There is a computer in your car that controls the engine. There is a computer in your cell phone. There is a computer in most cable or satellite television boxes. The things that they all have in common are that they all have a CPU and RAM. The differences are all in the peripherals. A cell phone has a small keyboard and screen, a microphone and a speaker, and a two-way radio for peripherals. Your car has various sensors and controls on the engine, and the dials of the dashboard for peripherals. The cash register in a fast food restaurant has a funny keyboard, a small display screen and a small printer for receipts. There are computers in some traffic lights that change the lights based on the time of day and the amount of traffic that crosses the sensors embedded in the roadway. But the CPU and RAM make it a computer, the peripherals can be very different.

For the rest of the book we will look at miscellaneous subjects related to understanding how computers are used, a few interesting words that are related to computers, some of their frailties and a few other loose ends.

Hardware and Software

You've heard of hardware. That word has been around for a long time. There have been hardware stores for a century or more. I think that a hardware store originally sold things that were hard, like pots and pans, screwdrivers, shovels, hammers, nails, plows, etc. Perhaps 'hardware' meant things that were made out of metal. Today, some hardware stores no longer sell pots and pans, but they sell huge variety of hard things, like bolts and lawnmowers, also lumber and a lot of soft things too, like carpet, wallpaper, paint, etc. But these soft things are not called software.

The word 'software' was invented somewhere in the early days of the computer industry to differentiate the computer itself from the state of the bits within it. Software means the way the bits are set on or off in a computer as opposed to the computer itself. Remember that bits can be either on or off. The bit has a location in space, it is made of something, it exists in space, it can be seen. The bit is hardware. Whether the bit is on or off is important, but it's not a separate part that you bolt into the computer, it is the thing in the computer that is changeable, the thing that can be molded, it is 'soft' in that it can change, but you can't pick it up in your hand all by itself. This thing is called software.

Think of a blank videotape. Then record a movie on it. What is the difference between the blank videotape and the same videotape with a movie on it? It looks the same, it weighs the same, you can't see any difference on the surface of the tape. That surface is coated with very fine particles that can be magnetized. In the blank tape, the entire surface of the tape is magnetized in random directions. After recording the movie on the tape, some little places on the tape are magnetized in one direction and other little places are magnetized in the other direction. Nothing is added to or taken away from the tape, it's just the way the magnetic particles are magnetized. When you put the tape into a VCR it plays a movie. The tape is hardware, the pattern of the directions of magnetization on the tape is software.

In a computer, there are a great many bits. As we have seen, a lot of bits have to be set in certain ways in order to make the computer do something useful. The bits in the computer are always there. If you want the computer to do a certain thing, you set those bits on or off according to the pattern that will make the computer do what you want it to do. This pattern is called software. It is not a physical thing, it is just the pattern in which the bits are set.

So the difference between hardware and software isn't like metal versus rubber. Both metal and rubber are hardware as far as the computer definition is concerned. Hardware is something you can pick up, see, handle. Software is the way the hardware is set. When you buy software, it is recorded on something, usually some kind of disk. The disk is hardware, the specific pattern recorded on that disk is software. Another disk may look just like it, but have completely different software written on it.

Another way to see the difference between hardware and software is how easy it is to send it across a distance. If you have a vase that you want to send to your aunt Millie for her birthday, you have to pack the vase in a box and have a truck take it from your house to her house. But if you want to give her the present of music, you might go to the store, buy her a disk and mail it, but you might also buy her a gift certificate on the Internet, send her an e-mail, and have her download the music. In that case, the music will get to her house without a truck having to go there. The music will be transported solely by the pattern of electricity that comes over the Internet connection to her house.

Another way to see the difference between hardware and software is how easy it is to make a copy of the item. If you have a lawnmower, and want a second lawnmower, there is no machine that will copy the lawnmower. You could photograph the lawnmower, but you'd only have a flat photograph of a lawnmower. You couldn't mow any lawns with the photo. To get a real second lawnmower, you'd have to go back to the lawnmower factory and build another one out of iron and plastic and rope and whatever else lawnmowers are made out of. This is hardware.

Software can be copied easily by machine. All you need is something that can read the disk or whatever it is recorded on, and something else to write it onto a new disk. The new one will be just like the original, it will do all the same things. If the original is your favorite movie, the copy will also be your favorite movie. If the original is a program that will prepare your tax papers, so will the copy.

Software is not a physical thing, it is just how the physical things are set.

By far the most commonly used definition of 'software' is to refer to a package of computer instruction code. I think that the way it got this name is that once you have built a device as versatile as a computer, there are many different things that it can be made to do. But when there are no instructions in it, it can't do anything. So the software is an absolutely necessary part of a computer that is doing some task. It is a vital part of the total machine, yet it isn't like any other part in the machine. You can't weigh it or measure it or pick it up with a pair of pliers. So it is part of the 'ware,' but it isn't hardware. The only thing left to call it is 'software.'

Programs

As mentioned earlier, a series of instructions in RAM are called a program.

Programs come in many sizes. Generally, a program is a piece of software that has everything needed to do a specific task. A system would be something larger, made up of several programs. A program might be made up of several smaller parts known as 'routines.' Routines in turn may be made up of sub-routines.

There are no hard and fast definitions that differentiate between system, program, routine and sub-routine. Program is the general term for all of them, the only difference is their size and the way they are used.

There is another distinction between two types of programs that is not related to their size. Most home and business computers have a number of programs installed on them. Most of these programs are used to do something that the owner wants to do. These are called application programs because they are written to apply the computer to a problem that needs to be solved. There is one program on most computers that is not an application. Its job is to deal with the computer itself and to assist the application programs. This one program that is not an application is called the Operating System.

The Operating System

An "Operating System," or "OS" for short, is a large program that has many parts and several objectives.

Its first job is to get the computer up and running when you first turn the computer on.

Another one of its jobs is to start and end application programs and give each one time to run. It is the 'boss' of every other program on that computer. When more than one program is in RAM, it is the operating system that switches between them. It lets one program run for a small fraction of a second, then another program, then another program. If there are ten programs in RAM, and each one gets to run for one hundredth of a second at a time, each program would be able to execute millions of instructions in that time, several times per second. It would appear that all ten programs were running simultaneously because each one gets to do something, faster than the eye can see.

An Operating system also provides services to application programs. When an application program needs to read from, or write to the disk, or draw letters on the screen, it does not have to do all of the complicated I/O instructions necessary to accomplish the task. The OS has a number of small routines that it keeps in RAM at all times for such purposes.

All an application needs to do to use one of these routines is to load up some information in the registers, and then jump to the address of the proper OS routine. Here's an example of how it might be done. Lets say you want to draw a character on the screen. First, put the ASCII code of the desired character into R0. Then put row and column numbers of where you want it to appear on the screen into R1 and R2. And here's the tricky part: You put the address of the next instruction of your application program, into R3. Now just jump to the OS routine. The routine will take care of all of the details of drawing the character on the screen, and then its last instruction will be JMPR R3. Thus, these routines can be 'called' from any application, and when done, the routine will jump back to the next instruction in the application that called it.

There are several reasons for having the OS do all of the I/O functions. One is that it makes it easier to write application programs, the programmer does not even need to know how the peripherals actually work. Another reason is that it would waste a lot of RAM if every application had its own copy of all of the I/O routines. One of the most important reasons is that the OS can check to see whether the program should be allowed to do what it is asking to do. This is part of the OS's other job of being the boss.

The heart of the OS is basically a loop of instructions that asks the following questions: Do I need to input anything? Do I need to output anything? Do I need to let any program run? Then it starts over again. If the answers to all of these questions is no, the CPU just executes the instructions in this loop over and over, millions of times per second. When there is something to do, it jumps to the beginning of the program that takes care of it, and when that is done, it jumps back to this loop where the OS 'waits' for something else to do.

Here is a diagram of our larger RAM version, showing what parts of RAM might be occupied by an Operating System and several other programs.

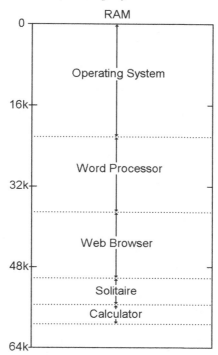

Within each program's RAM, there is all of the instruction code that makes the program work. Each program may be divided up into its own main loop, and many routines that are used for the various tasks that it needs to do. As mentioned, the OS also has routines that can be called by other programs.

Each program also uses part of its 'address space' for the data that it is working on. The calculator, for example, needs to have a few bytes where it stores the numbers that the user enters into it. Solitaire needs some bytes that specify which cards are in which positions. The word processor needs some RAM for all of the ASCII codes that make up the document you are working on. The OS also needs bytes where it can store fonts, keep track of where application programs have been loaded, receive the data that it reads from the disk, and for many other purposes.

And so this is what goes on inside your average computer. There are many different programs and data areas in RAM. The OS jumps to a program, the program jumps to a routine, the routine jumps to a sub-routine. Each program works on its data or calculates something or does an I/O operation. As each one finishes, it jumps back to where it came from. The CPU executes one instruction from one program at a time, and if they are written intelligently, each program will get its job done piece by piece, without interfering with the rest.

If our computer had included an 'interrupt system' like we described a few chapters back, every time someone pressed a key on the keyboard or moved the mouse, there would be an interrupt that would call a part of the OS that determines which I/O device caused the interrupt, and then calls the proper routine to take care of whatever it was. When that was done, the CPU would continue on with the next instruction of whatever program had been running when the interrupt happened.

This can all seem very complex, with so many millions and billions of instructions being executed in the blink of an eye. There are ways of organizing programs and good programming practices that can make it much more understandable. A study of these would simplify software in the same manner that I hope this book has simplified the hardware. But that would be the subject for another entire book.

Languages

Writing programs is very hard to do when you're just writing ones and zeros, but that is the only code that the CPU 'understands.'

What is a language? A spoken language, such as English, is a way to represent objects, actions and ideas with sounds. A written language is a way to represent the sounds of a spoken language with symbols on paper. Sounds like another code, and a code representing a code. We just can't get away from these things!

Do you remember that shorthand we used when we were looking at the CPU instruction code and the wiring in the Control Section? Well, that is actually something more than just a handy tool that was invented for this book. It is a computer language. Here are a few lines of it:

Instruction Code	Language		Meaning
1000 rarb	ADD	RA,RB	Add
1001 rarb	SHR	RA,RB	Shift Right
1010 rarb	SHL	RA,RB	Shift Left
1011 rarb	NOT	RA,RB	Not

A computer language is a way to represent the instruction code. Its purpose is to make it easier to write computer programs.

In order to use this language, you write the program you want with ASCII characters, and save it into a file. Then you load a special program called a 'compiler' into RAM and jump to its first instruction. The compiler will read the ASCII file, translate each line into the Instruction Code that it represents, and write all of the Instruction Code bytes into a second file. The second file may then be loaded into RAM, and when the CPU jumps to its first instruction, the program you wrote in ASCII will hopefully do what you intended it to do.

Of course, when computers were first invented, all programs had to be written directly in ones and zeros. Then somebody got tired of the tedium of programming that way, and decided to write the first compiler. Then ever after, programs were written in this easier language, and then translated into Instruction

Code by the compiler. With the original compiler, you could even write a better compiler.

So in order for a computer language to exist, you need two things, a set of words that make up the language (another code,) and a compiler that compiles the written language into computer instruction code.

The language that we have seen in this book has only about 20 words in it. Each word correlates directly to one of the instructions of which this computer is capable. Each line you write results in one computer instruction. When you write an 87 line program in this language, the instruction code file that the compiler generates will have 87 instructions in it.

Then someone invented a "higher level" language where one line of the language could result in multiple computer instructions. For example, our computer does not have an instruction that does subtraction. But the compiler could be designed so that it would recognize a new word in the language like 'SUB RA,RB' and then generate however many machine instructions were necessary to make the subtraction happen. If you can figure out how to do something fancy with 47 instructions, you can have a word in your language that means that fancy thing.

Then someone invented an even higher level language where the words that make up the language don't even resemble the CPU's actual instructions. The compiler has a lot more work to do, but still generates instruction code that does the things that the words in that language mean. A few lines from a higher level language might look like this:

    Balance = 2,000
    Interest Rate = .034
    Print "Hello Joe, your interest this year is: $"
    Print Balance X Interest Rate

The compiler for this language would read this four-line program, and generate a file that could easily contain hundreds of bytes of instruction code. When that instruction code was loaded into RAM and run, it would print:

    Hello Joe, your interest this year is: $68

Writing software in higher level languages can result in getting a lot more done in a shorter amount of time, and the programmer no longer needs to know exactly how the computer actually works.

There are many computer languages. Some languages are designed to do scientific work, some are designed for business purposes, others are more general purpose. Lower level languages are still the best for certain purposes.

The File System

As we saw earlier, the way a disk actually works is pretty foreign to most people who use a computer.

To make things easier, someone invented an idea called a "file." A file is supposed to be similar to the kind of paper files that people use in offices. A paper file is a sheet of cardboard folded in half and placed in a file cabinet. This folder has a tab on it where you can write some sort of name for the folder, and then you can put one or many pieces of paper in the folder.

A computer file is a string of bytes that can be any length, from one byte up to all of the bytes available on the disk. A file also has a name. A disk may have many files on it, each with its own name.

Of course, these files are just an idea. To make a file system work, the operating system provides a bunch of software that makes the disk appear to be like a filing cabinet instead of having heads, tracks, sectors and blocks of bytes.

This file system gives application programs an easy way of using the disk. Applications can ask the OS to create, read, write or erase something called a file. All the application needs to know is the name of the file. You open it, request bytes, send it bytes, make it bigger or smaller, close the file.

The OS uses part of the disk to maintain a list of file names, along with the length of each file and the disk address (head, track, sector) of the first sector of the data. If the file is smaller than a disk sector, that's all you need, but if the file is larger than one sector, then there is also a list which contains as many disk-type addresses as needed to hold the file.

The application program says create a file with the name "letter to Jane." Then the user types the letter to Jane and saves it. The program tells the OS where the letter is in RAM and how long it is, and the OS writes it to disk in the proper sector or sectors and updates the file length and any necessary lists of disk-type addresses.

To use the file system, there will be some sort of rules that the application program needs to follow. If you want to write some bytes to the disk, you would need to tell the OS the name of the file, the RAM address of the bytes that you want to write, and how many bytes to write. Typically, you would put all of this information in a series of bytes somewhere in RAM, and then put the RAM address of the first byte of this information in one of the registers, and then execute a Jump instruction that jumps to a routine within the Operating System that writes files to the disk. All of the details are taken care of by this routine, which is part of the OS.

If you ask the OS to look at your disk, it will show you a list of all the file names, and usually their sizes and the date and time when they were last written to.

You can store all sorts of things in files. Files usually have names that are made up of two parts separated by a period like "xxxx.yyy." The part before the period is some sort of a name like "letter to Jane," and the part after the dot is some sort of a type like "doc" which is short for "document." The part before the period tells you something about what is in the file. The part after the dot tells you what type of data is contained in this file, in other words, what code it uses.

The type of the file tells both you and the OS what code the data in the file uses. In one popular operating system ".txt" means text, which means that the file contains ASCII. A ".bmp" means BitMaP, which is a picture. A ".exe" means executable, which means it is a program and therefore contains Instruction Code.

If you ask the OS what programs are available to execute, it will show you a list of the files that end with ".exe". If you ask for a list of pictures that you can look at, it will show you a list of files that end with ".bmp".

There are many possible file types, any program can invent its own type, and use any code or combination of codes.

Errors

The computer is a fairly complex machine that does a series of simple things one after another very quickly. What sorts of things could go wrong here?

In the early days of computing, when each gate in the computer was relatively expensive to build, sometimes there were components that actually had moving parts to make electrical connections. Two pieces of metal had to touch to make the electricity go to where the builders wanted it to go. Sometimes when the machine stopped working correctly, the fixit guy would look inside to find out what was wrong, and he would find that a spider had crawled inside the machine and had gotten itself wedged in between two of these pieces of metal that were supposed to touch each other. Then when one piece of metal moved to touch the other, the spider was in the way and they wouldn't touch. So the electricity wouldn't get to where it needed to go, and the machine would not operate correctly anymore. The fixit guy would remove the bug, clean up the contacts, and report "There was a bug in the computer." And he literally meant a bug.

Over time, whenever a computer appeared to be operating incorrectly, people would say that the computer had a bug. There are two main classes of computer bugs: hardware and software.

A hardware bug actually means that the computer is broken. This could be as serious as you turn the computer on, and it catches fire, to there is one byte in the RAM where one bit is always off.

Now one bit in RAM that refuses to change may be a problem or it may not. If the byte where that bit is located somehow never gets used, then the computer will work just fine. If that byte is part of a place where a name is stored, then the name may get changed from "Joe" to "Jod." If that byte has some program instructions in it, you may get an XOR instruction changed to a JMP instruction. Then when the program gets to that instruction, it will not do the XOR like it is supposed to, but rather it will jump somewhere else and start executing whatever is at the new location as though it was a series of instructions. The contents of those bytes will determine what happens next, but it will almost certainly be as wrong as a train falling off its track.

If a gate is broken in the stepper, for instance, so that step 4 never comes on, then the computer will not really be able to operate at all. It would still be able to fetch instructions in steps 1, 2 and 3, but every instruction would execute incorrectly. Certainly the program would make a mess of things after 'executing' just a few instructions.

Software bugs can take many forms, but they are all ultimately programmer mistakes. There are probably many more ways to write a program incorrectly than correctly. Some errors just create some kind of incorrect results, and other errors cause the computer to "crash."

One of my favorite stupid programmer stories is this: Someone bought a car on credit. He got a coupon book with the loan, one coupon to be sent in with each payment. But when he made his first payment, he accidentally used the last coupon in the book instead of the first one. A few weeks later, he received a computer-generated letter from the loan company saying, "Thank you for paying off your loan in full, next time you need a loan please use us again." Obviously, the program just checked the coupon number and if it was equal to the highest number coupon in the book, jump to the routine for a paid-in-full loan. It should have at least checked the balance remaining on the loan before deciding that it was paid off. This is a subtle error, it might not be caught by the loan company until they audited their books months later. The computer did exactly what it was told to do, and most of the time it was adequate, but the program was not written to anticipate all of the situations that sometimes occur in the real world.

One of the worst software bugs is getting stuck in a loop. The program executes a series of instructions, and then jumps back to the beginning of the series and executes it over and over again. Of course, loops are used all the time in programming, but they are used to do something that has a finite number of similar steps. It may repeat until 50 bytes have been moved somewhere, or keep checking for the user to press a key on the keyboard. But the computer will exit the loop at some point and continue on to its next task. But if there is some sort of programming error where there is a loop that has no way out, the computer will appear to be completely stuck. This is sometimes called being 'hung,' the whole computer may need to be turned off and restarted to get out of the loop and back into useful operation.

There are all sorts of errors that end up with the CPU trying to execute something other than instruction code. Lets say you have your program residing at address 10 through 150, and you have some ASCII data such as names and phone numbers at addresses 151 through 210. If the program is written incorrectly so that under certain conditions it will jump to address 180, it will just continue fetching and executing the bytes starting at address 180. If 180-189 was filled with the ASCII for "Jane Smith," the "program" will now be executing complete garbage, a series of bytes that were not designed to be Instruction Code. It may put itself into a loop, or jump back somewhere into the program, or issue the command to erase the disk drive. And it will be doing garbage at its usual high speed. If you looked at the patterns in the bytes, you could see what it would do, but it could be just about anything. If the name at address 180 was "Bill Jones", it would do something completely different. Since it is not designed to be useful, most likely it will just keep making a bigger mess out of what is in memory until the computer will have to be powered off to get it to stop.

Another type of error could occur if a program accidentally wrote "John Smith" into the place where a font was stored. In that case, every letter "E" that got drawn on the screen thereafter would look like this: '⅊.'

The computer executes hundreds of millions of instructions every second, and it only takes one wrong instruction to bring the whole thing to a screeching halt. Therefore, the subject of programming computers in a manner that will be completely 'bug free' is something that gets a lot of attention. Almost all programming is done with languages, and the compilers for these languages are designed to generate Instruction Code that avoids the most serious types of errors, and to warn the programmer if certain good programming practices are violated. Still, compilers can have errors, and they will never be able to spot an error like the one above with the car loan.

As you can see, the computer and its software are pretty fragile things. Every gate has to work every time, and every instruction that gets executed has to be correct. When you consider all of the things that could go wrong, the high percentage of things that normally go right is actually quite impressive.

Computer Diseases?

Another place where human characteristics get assigned to computers is something called a computer virus. This implies that computers can come down with a disease and get sick. Are they going to start coughing and sneezing? Will they catch a cold or the chicken pox? What exactly is a computer virus?

A computer virus is a program written by someone who wants to do something bad to you and your computer. It is a program that will do some sort of mischief to your computer when it runs. The motivation of people who write virus programs ranges from the simple technical challenge of seeing whether one is capable of doing it, to a desire to bring down the economy of the whole world. In any case, the people who do such things do not have your best interests in mind.

How does a computer 'catch' a virus? A virus program has to be placed in your RAM, and your computer has to jump to the virus program and run it. When it runs, it locates a file that is already on your hard disk, that contains a program that gets run on a regular basis by your computer, like some part of the operating system. After the virus program locates this file, it copies the virus program to the end of this file, and inserts a jump instruction at the beginning of the file that causes a jump to where the virus program is. Now your computer has a virus.

When a computer with a virus is running, it does all of the things it is supposed to do, but whenever it runs the program that contains the virus, the inserted jump instruction causes the virus program to be run instead. Now the virus usually will do something simple, like check for a predetermined date, and if it is not a match, then the virus program will jump back to the beginning of the file where the operating system program still exists.

Thus, your computer will appear totally normal, there are just a few extra instructions being executed during its regular operations. The virus is considered dormant at this point. But when that date arrives, and the virus 'decides' to do whatever is in the rest of its program, it can be anything. When the virus program is running, it can do whatever mischief the person who wrote it could think of. It can erase files on your disk, or send them somewhere else via the internet. One humorous virus would, every once in a while, make the letters on the screen appear to come loose and fall into a pile at the bottom of the screen.

Here's an example of how to catch a virus. Let's say that you have a friend who finds a funny movie on the Internet. It makes him laugh, and he thinks that you will enjoy it too, so he emails the movie file to you. You receive the movie file and play it, and you do enjoy it.

There are two different things that could have occurred here. If your friend sent you a file named "funny.mov," and your OS includes a program that plays '.mov' files, then the OS will load that program into RAM, and that program will read the pictures in the "funny.mov" file and display them on your screen. This is fine, the program that ran was something that was already on your computer. The "funny.mov" file just provided a series of pictures that were displayed on your screen.

But if your friend sent you a file named "funny.exe," then when you ask the OS to play the movie, it will load "funny.exe" into RAM and jump to its first instruction. Now you have a program running in your computer that came from somewhere else. If it is a virus program, it will probably play the movie for you so that you don't suspect anything, but it can do anything else that it wants, to the files on your disk while you are watching the movie. It will probably install itself and go into a dormant state for days or weeks, and you won't even know that your computer is 'infected.' But sooner or later it will come alive and do whatever damage it was designed to do.

This sort of malicious program is called a virus because the way it works is similar to the way that real viruses infect living things. A real virus is a thing that is smaller than a one celled animal. It doesn't quite qualify as being alive because the virus by itself cannot reproduce. They do reproduce, however, by invading a cell of something that is alive. Once in the cell, the virus uses the mechanisms of that cell to make copies of itself, which can then go on and infect other cells.

The computer virus also cannot reproduce or do anything else by itself. It needs to get into a computer, and somehow get itself executed one time by that CPU. When it runs that first time, it inserts itself somewhere into the operating system so that it will thereafter get executed on a regular basis. Those instructions will do whatever damage they are designed to do to the computer on which they are running, and they will also usually do something that is designed to spread the virus to other computers.

Firmware

Of course, RAM is an essential part of any computer. The ability to write bytes into RAM, and read them back out again is an integral part of how the machine works.

But in some computers, there are sections of the RAM that only get written to when the computer starts up, and thereafter these sections remain unchanged as the computer operates. This could be true in any computer that always runs the same program. Perhaps half of the RAM is used to contain the program, and the other half of the RAM is used to contain the data that the program is working on. The half with the program has to be loaded at some point, but after that, the CPU only has to read the bytes of the program in order to fetch and execute them.

When you have this sort of situation, you can build half of your computer's RAM the normal way, and with the other half, you skip the NAND gates, and just wire each bit directly to an on or an off in the pattern of your program.

Of course, you can't write into the pre-wired RAM, but you can read from it just fine. This type of RAM was given the name Read Only Memory, or ROM for short. You use it the same way you use RAM, but you only read from it.

There are two advantages to ROM. In the early days of computers, when RAM was very expensive, ROM was a lot less expensive than RAM.

The other advantage is that you no longer have to load the program into RAM when you first turn the computer on. It is already there in ROM, ready to be executed by the CPU.

The point here is a new word. Since software was named 'soft' because it is changeable, when it comes to ROM, you still have a pattern in the bits, but they're not so soft anymore. You can't write into a ROM, you can't change the bits. And so this type of memory came to be known as 'firmware.' It is software that is permanently written into hardware.

But that isn't the end of the story. The ROM described above had to be built that way at the factory. Over the years, this idea was improved and made easier to use.

The next advance was when someone had the bright idea of making ROM where every bit was set on at the factory, but there was a way of writing to it with a lot of power that could burn out individual connections, changing individual bits to an off. Thus this ROM could be programmed after leaving the factory. This was called 'Programmable ROM' or 'PROM' for short.

Then someone figured out how to make a PROM that would repair all of those broken connections if it were exposed to ultraviolet light for a half an hour. This was called an 'Erasable PROM', or 'EPROM' for short.

Then someone figured out how to build an EPROM that could be erased by using extra power on a special wire built into the EPROM. This was called 'Electrically Erasable PROM', or 'EEPROM' for short. One particular type of EEPROM has the name 'Flash memory.'

So there is RAM, ROM, PROM, EPROM, EEPROM and Flash. These are all types of computer memory. The thing they have in common is that they all allow random access. They all work the same way when it comes to addressing bytes and reading out the data that is in them. The big difference is that RAM loses its settings when the power goes off. When the power comes back on, RAM is full of all zeros. The rest of them all still have their data after power off and back on.

You may ask then, "Why don't computers use EEPROM for their RAM? Then the program would stay in RAM when the computer was off." The answer is that it takes much longer to write into EEPROM than RAM. It would slow the computer down tremendously. If someone figures out how to make an EEPROM that is as fast and as cheap and uses the same or less power as RAM, I'm sure it will be done.

By the way, the word ROM has also come to be used to mean any type of storage that is permanently set, such as a pre recorded disk, as in 'CD ROM,' but its original definition only applied to something that worked just like RAM.

Boots

What do boots have to do with computers? Well, there is an old phrase that goes "pull yourself up by your own bootstraps." It is kind of a joke, it literally refers to the straps that are sewn into many boots that are used to help pull the boots onto your feet. The joke is that if you are wearing such a pair of boots, and want to get up off the ground, instead of getting a ladder or climbing a rope, you can get yourself off the ground by simply pulling hard enough on those bootstraps. Of course this would only work in a cartoon, but the phrase has come to mean doing something when there is no apparent way to do it, or doing something without the tools that would normally be used, or accomplishing something by yourself without help from anyone else.

In a computer, there is a problem that is similar to needing to get off the ground and having no tools available to accomplish it. When a computer is operating, the memory is full of programs that are doing something, and when the operator of the computer enters a command to start another program, the operating system locates the program on disk, loads it into memory, and jumps to the first instruction of the program. Now that program is running.

But when you first turn on a computer, how do you get the operating system into memory? It takes a program running in memory to tell the disk drive to send over some instruction code, and the program needs to write that code into memory at an appropriate place, and then jump to its first instruction to get the new program running. But when you turn the computer on, every byte in memory is all zeros. There are no instructions in memory at all. This is the impossible situation, you need a program in memory to get a program in memory, but there is nothing there. So in order for the computer to get going in the first place, the computer has to do something impossible. It has to pull itself up by its bootstraps!

A long time ago, in the early days of computers, the machine had switches and push buttons on the front panel that allowed the operator to enter bytes of data directly into the registers, and from there, into RAM. You could manually enter a short program this way, and start it running. This program, called a "bootstrap loader," would be the smallest possible program you could write that would instruct the computer to read bytes from a peripheral, store them in RAM, and then jump to the first instruction. When the bootstrap loader executes, it loads a much larger program into memory, such as the beginnings of an operating system, and then the computer will become usable.

Nowadays, there are much easier ways of loading the first program into the computer, in fact it happens automatically immediately after the computer gets turned on. But this process still happens, and the first step is called "booting" or "booting up" and it only means getting the first program into memory and beginning to execute it.

The most common solution to this problem has three parts. First, the IAR is designed so that when the power is first turned on, instead of all of its bits being zero, its last bit will be zero, but the rest of its bits will be ones. Thus for our little computer, the first instruction to be fetched will be at address 1111 1110. Second, something like the last 32 bytes of the RAM (235-256) will be ROM instead, hardwired with a simple program that accesses the disk drive, selects head 0, track 0, sector 0, reads this sector into RAM, and then jumps to the first byte of it. The third part then, had better be that there is a program written on that first sector of the disk. This sector, by the way, is called the 'boot record.'

This word 'boot' has become a verb in computer talk. It means to load a program into RAM where there are no programs. Sometimes people use it to mean loading any program into RAM, but its original meaning only applied to loading the first program into an otherwise blank RAM.

Digital vs. Analog

You've no doubt heard these terms bandied about. It seems that anything associated with computers is digital, and everything else is not. But that's not quite close enough to the truth.

What they mean is quite simple, but where they came from and how they ended up in their current usage is not so straightforward.

The word 'digital' comes from digit, which means fingers and toes in some ancient language, and since fingers and toes have been used for counting, digital means having to do with numbers. Today, the individual symbols that we use to write numbers (0, 1, 2, 3, etc.) are called digits. In the computer, we represent numbers with bits and bytes. One of the qualities of bits and bytes is their unambiguous nature. A bit is either on or off; there is no gray area in between. A byte is always in one of its 256 states; there is no state between two numbers like 123 and 124. The fact that these states change in steps is what we are referring to when we say digital.

The word 'analog' comes from the same place as 'analogy' and 'analogous,' thus it has to do with the similarity between two things. In the real world, most things change gradually and continuously, not in steps. A voice can be a shout or a whisper or absolutely anywhere in between. When a telephone converts a voice into an electrical equivalent so that it can travel through a wire to another telephone, that electricity can also vary everywhere between being fully on and fully off. Sound and electricity are two very different things, but the essence of the voice has been duplicated with electricity. Since they are similar in that respect, we can say that the electrical pattern is an 'analog' of the voice. Although the meaning of 'analog' comes from this 'similarity' factor, when you make an analog, you are usually making an analog of something that is continuously variable. This idea of something being continuously variable has come to be the definition of analog when you are comparing digital and analog. Something that is analog can be anywhere within the entirety of some range, there are no steps.

Digital means change by steps and analog means change in a smooth continuous manner. Another way to say it is that digital means that the elements that make up a whole come from a finite number of choices, whereas analog means that a thing is made of parts that can be selected from an unlimited number of choices. A few non-computer examples may help to clarify this.

If you have a platform that is three feet above the floor, you can either build stairs for people to climb up to it, or a ramp. On the ramp, you can climb to any level between the floor and the platform; on the stairs, you only have as many choices as there are steps. The ramp is analog, the stairs are digital.

Let's say that you want to build a walkway in your garden. You have a choice of making the walkway out of concrete or out of bricks. If the bricks are three inches wide, then you can make a brick walk that is 30 inches wide, or 33 inches wide, but not 31 or 32. If you make the walk out of concrete, you can pour it to any width you want. The bricks are digital, the concrete is analog.

If you have an old book and an old oil painting, and you want to make a copy of each, you will have a much easier time making a copy of the book. Even if the pages of the book are yellowed, and the corners are dog-eared, and there are dirt smudges and worm holes inside, as long as you can read every letter in the book, you could re-type the entire text, exactly as the author intended it. With the oil painting, the original colors may have faded and are obscured by dirt. The exact placement of each bristle in each brush stroke, the thickness of the paint at every spot, the way adjacent colors mix, could all be copied in great detail, but there would inevitably be some slight differences. Each letter in the book comes from a list of a specific number of possibilities; the variations of paint colors and their positions on the canvas are limitless. The book is digital, the painting is analog.

So there you have the difference between analog and digital. The world around us is mostly analog. Most old technologies were analog, like the telephone, phonograph, radio, television, tape recorders and videocassettes. Oddly enough though, one of the oldest devices, the telegraph, was digital. Now that digital technology has become highly developed and inexpensive, the analog devices are being replaced one by one with digital versions that accomplish the same things.

Sound is an analog thing. An old fashioned telephone is an analog machine that converts analog sound into an electrical pattern that is an analog of the sound, which then travels through a wire to another phone. A new digital telephone takes the analog sound, and converts it into a digital code. Then the digital code travels to another digital phone where the digital code is converted back into analog sound.

Why would anyone go to the trouble of inventing a digital phone when the analog phone worked just fine? The answer, of course, is that although the analog phone worked, it was not perfect. When an analog electrical pattern travels over long distances, many things can happen to it along the way. It gets smaller and smaller as it travels, so it has to be amplified, which introduces noise, and when it gets close to other electrical equipment, some of the pattern from the other equipment can get mixed in to the conversation. The farther the sound goes, the more noise and distortion are introduced. Every change to the analog of your voice becomes a part of the sound that comes out at the other end.

Enter digital technology to the rescue. When you send a digital code over long distances, the individual bits are subjected to the same types of distortion and noise, and they do change slightly. However, it doesn't matter if a bit is only 97% on instead of 100%. A gate's input only needs to 'know' whether the bit is on or off, it has to 'decide' between those two choices only. As long as a bit is still more than half way on, the gate that it goes into will act in exactly the same way as if the bit had been fully on. Therefore, the digital pattern at the end is just as good as it was at the beginning, and when it is converted back to analog, there is no noise or distortion at all, it sounds like the person is right next-door.

There are advantages and disadvantages to each method, but in general, the benefits of digital technology far outweigh its shortcomings.

Probably the biggest advantage of digital has to do with the making of copies. When you make a copy of something like a vinyl record, you could record it to a tape recorder, or I guess you could even get all of the equipment to cut a new vinyl record. But there will be some degree of difference between the original and the copy. In the first place, all machinery has accuracy limitations. A copy of any physical object can be very close to the original, but never quite exact. Second, if there are any scratches or particles of dust on the original, the copy will then have duplicates of these defects. Third, friction between the record and the needle actually wears away a tiny amount of vinyl every time you play it. If you use a tape recorder, there is always a low level of 'hiss' added to the sound. If you make a copy of a copy, and a copy of that, etc. the changes will get larger and larger at each stage.

When it comes to something that is digital, as long as every bit that was on in the original is also on in the copy, we get an exact copy every time. You can make a copy of the copy, and a copy of that, etc., and every one of them will be exactly the same as the original. Digital is definitely the way to go if you want to be able to make an unlimited number of copies and preserve something for all time.

The computer and peripherals we have built are entirely digital so far. And if all we ever wanted to do with them were digital things such as arithmetic and written language, we could leave it that way. However, if we want our computer to play music and work with color photographs, there is one more thing we need to look at.

I Lied – Sort of

There is one piece of hardware in a computer that is not made completely out of NAND gates. This thing is not really necessary to make a computer a computer, but most computers have a few of them. They are used to change from something that is analog to something that is digital, or digital to analog.

Human eyes and ears respond to analog things. Things that we hear can be loud or soft, things that we see can be bright or dark and be any of a multitude of colors.

The computer display screen that we described above had 320 x 200 or 64,000 pixels. But each pixel only had one bit to tell it what to do, to be on or off. This is fine for displaying written language on the screen, or it could be used to make line drawings, anything that only has two levels of brightness. But we have all seen photographs on computer screens.

First of all, there needs to be a way to put different colors on the screen. If you get out a magnifying glass and look at a color computer or television screen, you will see that the screen is actually made up of little dots of three different colors, blue, red, and green. Each pixel has three parts to it, one for each color. When the display adapter scans the screen, it selects all three colors of each pixel at the same time.

For a computer to have a color screen, it needs to have three bits for each pixel, so it would have to have three times the RAM in order to be able to control the three colors in each pixel individually. With three bits, each color could be fully on or off, and each pixel would therefore have eight possible states: black, green, red, blue, green and red (yellow,) green and blue (cyan,) blue and red (magenta) and green, blue and red (white.)

But this is still not enough to display a photograph. To do that, we need to be able to control the brightness of each color throughout the range between fully on and fully off. To do this, we need a new type of part that we will describe shortly, and we need more bits in the display RAM. Instead of one bit for each color in each pixel, we could have a whole byte for each color in each pixel. That's three bytes per pixel, for a total of 192,000 bytes of RAM just for this small display screen.

With these bytes, using the binary number code, you could specify 256 levels of brightness for each color in each pixel. This would amount to 16,777,216 different states (or colors) for each pixel. This is enough variety to display a reasonably good-looking photograph.

In order to make this work – a number specifying 256 different levels of brightness – you need a thing called a "digital to analog converter" or "DAC" for short. A DAC has eight digital inputs, and one analog output. The way it works is that it is wired up to treat the input as a binary number, and the output has 256 levels between off and on. The output has 256 gradations between off and on, and it goes to the level that the input number specifies. If the input is a 128, the output will be halfway on. For a 64 the output will be one quarter on. For 0, the output will be fully off.

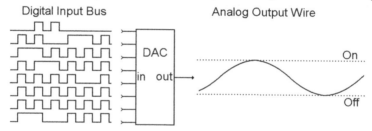

In order to make this color screen work, the display adapter needs to access three bytes at a time, connect them to three DACs, and connect the outputs of the DACs to the three colors in the current pixel being painted. That's how a color screen works.

When we defined 'analog' in the last chapter, we said that it was something that was continuously variable from fully off to fully on. But our DAC really only has 256 different levels at its 'analog' output. It's a lot closer to being analog than a bit, but it still has steps. What the computer is doing is approximating an analog thing in steps small enough to fool the intended audience. When it comes to the eye, 256 different levels of brightness is sufficient.

If something requires smaller steps to fool the intended audience, you can make a DAC that has 16 bits on the digital side. Thus you can present the digital input with a number anywhere from 0 to 65535. The analog side can still only vary from fully off to fully on, but the size of the steps will be much smaller since there are now 65536 of them.

When it comes to the ear, it can hear very small differences, and so a 16 bit DAC is required for high quality sound.

All sounds, from music to speech to thunder crashes are vibrations of the air. They vary in how fast the air vibrates, and in exactly how it vibrates. The human ear can hear vibrations from about 20 Hz at the low end to 20,000 Hz (20 kHz) at the high end, so this is the range of vibrations that computers are designed to deal with. For any electronic machine to make sounds, there is a device called a speaker. All that a speaker does is move back and forth in the air, making the air vibrate. If it makes the air vibrate in precisely the same way as the original thing that was recorded, it will sound just like the original.

In order to store a sound in a computer, the position of the speaker is divided into 65536 possible positions. Then a second is divided into 44,100 parts. At each one of those parts of a second, the desired position of the speaker is stored as a two-byte number. This is enough information to reproduce sound with very high quality.

To play top quality stereo music, a computer would need a 'sound peripheral.' This would have two 16 bit DACs with their analog outputs connected to speakers. It would also have its own clock that ticks at 44,100 Hz. At each tick, it would get the next two two-byte numbers, and connect them to the digital side of the DACs.

As far as speed goes, this would be 176,400 bytes per second. Certainly that is fast, but remember that our computer clock ticks a billion times per second. That means that the computer can send four bytes to the sound peripheral, and go off and execute about 4000 instructions on some other task before it needs to send the next four.

For going the other way, there is an "Analog to Digital Converter," or "ADC" for short. This is used to convert the sound from a microphone into a series of bytes, or for a camera to convert a picture into a series of bytes. The input has one wire that can be anywhere from all the way off to all the way on. The ADC makes its outputs into a number from 0-255 for an 8-bit ADC or from 0-65,535 for a 16-bit ADC. This number represents how much the input is on or off. Half on is 128 or 32,768, one quarter on is 64 or 16,384, etc. This process is just the reverse of what a DAC does.

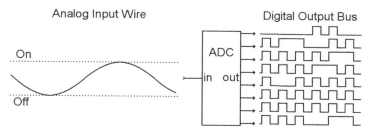

DACs and ADCs are not made out of NAND gates, they have electronic parts like radios have. How they do what they do is not a proper subject for this book. So maybe I lied when I said that everything in a computer is made out of NAND gates? Well, not really, because DACs and ADCs are only used in certain types of peripherals, not in the computer itself.

Full Disclosure

We have built a very small computer here. It is about the smallest computer that could be invented that does everything necessary to be worthy of the name computer. I don't think that anyone has built such a small computer since about 1952, and no one has ever built this exact computer in the real world.

If a real computer designer ever read this book, I'm sure he'd be pulling his hair out over all of the opportunities that have been missed here to make a better machine. But again, the goal has been to illustrate computer principles as simply as possible.

This is an eight-bit computer. That means that the registers in the processor are eight bits, the bus is eight bits, and in this machine, even the Memory Address Register is eight bits.

With most of the computers that actually get built, while the individual bytes in RAM remain 8 bits, everything else is expanded to 16 bits, 32 bits or 64 bits or a combination of these in different parts of the machine.

Our RAM only has 256 bytes, which is ridiculously small, but that's all you can have with an eight-bit Memory Address Register. If you use 16 bits, you can have 65,536 bytes of RAM (that's 64kb), if you use 24 bits you can have 16mb, if you use 32 bits you can have 4 gigabytes of RAM.

Real computers have things that this one does not, but they are not capable of doing things that this computer cannot do.

In our computer, if you want to shift a byte three bits to the left, you would put three shift left instructions in your program. In most real computers, they have shifters that will shift any number of bits in one instruction. But the result is the same, your byte ends up looking the same in either case, the real computer just gets the job done faster.

In our computer, the adder can add two eight-bit numbers. If you want to add 16 bit numbers, you have to employ some software to do it. In most computers, the adder can add 16 or 32 bit numbers in one instruction. Again, the results are the same, one is just faster than the other.

The stepper in our computer is a simplification of something that most computers have, called a 'state machine.' State machines provide steps, but start the next instruction as soon as possible, do what is necessary for an interrupt system, can create more complex instructions, etc. Since all we needed was six consecutive steps, we built a simpler thing and just made up the term 'stepper.'

So yes, our computer is a simple, small, relatively slow computer, but it can do everything that more complicated machines can do. The things that make a bigger machine bigger, are designed to get the job done faster, do it in fewer clock cycles, do the same task with fewer instructions, operate on several bytes at the same time. But the nature of what the machines do is exactly the same. Every task they can do comes down to shifting, ANDing, ORing, XORing, ADDing and NOTing bytes. There are no other fancy types of operations that have been left out of this book.

In a bigger machine, you can do addition, subtraction, multiplication and division in a single instruction. That is because they have huge numbers of gates arranged into things like a 'hardware multiplier.' There is no reason to show you the details of how you construct one of these, it is a very complicated job for the few people who need to build one. It is understandable, and it all ultimately comes down to NAND gates just like everything else. But we have seen how to do all the math operations there are with just an adder, shifter, NOT gates and some software. The hardware multiplier gets there faster, but the results are exactly the same.

Bigger machines have more registers, the registers are each multiple bytes, they have adders that can add three numbers at the same time, but still the instructions come down to the same simple operations. Your understanding of computers is not small because we have looked at a small computer.

Philosophy

Why do we have a chapter called "Philosophy" in a book about computers? The only thing in this book that even comes close to being a philosophical question is its title, "But How do it Know?" We will attempt to answer this question a little later on.

This book has been about the computers that we have today. But what about the future? As computers and software continue to advance, how soon if ever, will the day come when there are walking talking computerized robots that look and act just like people? Will the day come when we have to decide whether or not to give these robots the same legal rights as people? Will computers eventually take over the world and replace people altogether?

To answer these sorts of questions, people often refer to a major question that has been outstanding in the field of philosophy for many years.

The question is, whether man is composed solely of the structural body that we can see and dissect, or whether there is an integral spiritual component to every human being which accounts for the qualities of consciousness, love, honor, happiness, pain, etc.

That question is far beyond the scope of this book, and it remains unconvincingly answered despite many books arguing each viewpoint. There are people in the sciences who say that we are on track to building conscious computers, and it will happen. There are people in the humanities who say that it is impossible because you can't manufacture a spirit. Each side has been unable to sway the other.

If we define the brain as that funny looking chunk of gray meat enclosed by the skull, and define the mind as whatever it is that is responsible for consciousness, memory, creativity, thinking, and everything else that we notice going on in our heads, then we can restate the big philosophic question as: "Are the brain and the mind one and the same thing?"

Then when it comes to the question about building a convincing human robot, there would be two possibilities.

If the brain and the mind are the same thing, you might not be able to build a synthetic person today, but as time went on, eventually you could understand every structure and function in the brain, and build something of equal complexity that would generate true consciousness, and that really should act just like any other person.

If the brain and the mind are not the same thing, then building a robot buddy will always be about simulating humanity, not building something of equal quality and value.

Restating the question doesn't make it any easier to answer, but this idea of separating what we know about minds from what we know about brains may be useful. Early on, we said that we were going to show how computers work so that we could see what they were capable of doing, and also what they were not capable of doing. We are going to take what we know about brains and what we know about minds and compare each individually to our new knowledge about computers. In doing so we can look for differences and similarities, and we may be able to answer a few less controversial questions.

Computers do certain things with great ease, such as adding up columns of numbers. A computer can do millions of additions in a single second. The mind can barely remember two numbers at the same time, never mind adding them up without a pencil and paper.

The mind seems to have the ability to look at and consider relatively large amounts of data at the same time. When I think of my favorite cat, I can re-experience seeing what he looks like, hearing the sounds of his purring and mewing, feeling the softness of his fur and his weight when picked up. These are some of the ways that I know my pet.

What would it mean for our computer to think about a cat? It could have pictures of the cat and sounds of the cat encoded in files on a spinning disk or in RAM. Is that thinking? If you ran the bytes of these files one by one through the ALU, would that be thinking? If you put the picture on the screen, would that be thinking? If you played the sounds to the speakers, would that be thinking?

The sounds and pictures encoded in the computer are just byte patterns sitting where they are. They don't look like anything or sound like anything unless they are sent to the peripherals for which they were designed. And if they are sent to the screen and speakers, the computer doesn't see them or hear them. Of course, your computer could have a camera pointing at the screen, and a microphone listening to the sounds, but the computer still wouldn't see a picture or hear a sound, it would just collect more strings of bytes very similar to the ones sent to the screen and speakers in the first place.

There could be programs that perform mathematical operations on the picture files in order to discover patterns, and store the results of these calculations in other files. There could be files that relate one picture file to other similar picture files, and pictures to sounds, etc., creating more files.

But no matter how much programming is applied to the picture files, there is something that the mind can do that the computer simply doesn't have any facility for.

The mind can consider the whole of some thing all at the same time. You can think of the whole of the cat all at once. Its sort of like the difference between the movie film and the TV screen. The movie film has whole pictures, the TV screen only has one pixel at a time. You could say that your mind works so quickly that you don't notice the details, it gets integrated into a whole just like the pixels get integrated into an entire picture. But what does the integrating? And when it's integrated, what is it and where is it? And what looks at the integrated whole?

We've just seen everything that's in a computer. The computer moves one byte at a time over the bus. The fanciest thing it does is to add two bytes into one. Everything else it 'does' amounts to nothing more than the simple warehousing of bytes. A stored byte doesn't do anything beyond maintaining its own current setting. A computer just doesn't have any facilities that integrate the elements of a picture into anything else, nowhere to store that something else, and nothing with which to look at it.

I'm not saying that something couldn't be built that would perform these functions, I'm just saying that computers as we know them today don't currently include any such device.

Here is another question. If a brain works like a computer, then it needs to have a program for the CPU to run. Where would this program come from?

Although the brain has trillions of cells, the entire human body starts with one fertilized egg cell. So any program that the brain has, would have to be present in this single cell, presumably in the DNA.

Scientists have now decoded the entire DNA sequence of humans. DNA is interesting in that it is a long string of only four types of things. It's digital! A lot of the pieces of this string are used for making chemical reactions take place to make proteins, etc. but the majority of it is called 'junk DNA' because no one knows what its purpose is. But even if you consider that the entirety of the DNA is devoted to computer software, then there could be about a billion instructions in this program. Now that's a lot of software, but the average home computer probably has that much software loaded onto it's hard drive, and that wouldn't be anywhere near enough to run a human being.

Some have said that the human computer programs itself. As a programmer myself, I just can't imagine how this would work. While it's true that a program can accumulate data and modify the way it works based on the collected data, this is not the same thing as writing a new program. If someone ever writes this program that can write any new needed program, there will be a huge number of computer programmers put out of work forever.

Then there are the kinds of errors that computers make versus the kind that people make. If a computer gets stuck in a loop, it appears to have stopped completely. Have you ever seen a person walking down the street suddenly stop working? All functions just cease. The person would just fall down until somehow his computer re-booted. People do collapse from time to time, but it is usually because some other part broke, like having a heart attack, and you can see the person recognize the pain as it takes them down. But if the human computer got stuck in a loop, there would be an instant loss of consciousness and the body would just fall completely limp with no struggle. I have never seen that, but if the brain operated just like a computer, you would expect to see it on a fairly regular basis.

Then there is the matter of speed. As we have seen, a simple computer can do a billion things in a second. When it comes to the brain, it has nerves that have some similarity to the wires in computers. Nerves can also carry electricity from place to place. In a computer, wires come out of gates and go into other gates. In the brain, nerves are connected together by "synapses." These synapses are spaces between nerves where the electricity in one nerve creates a chemical reaction, which then causes the next nerve to create its own electricity. These chemical reactions are painfully slow.

No one has shown that these nerves are connected up anything like the wires in a computer, but their lack of speed makes it very unlikely that it would do much good even if the connections were similar. After the electricity travels quickly through the nerve cell, it reaches the synapse, where the chemical reaction takes about one five hundredth of a second to complete. That means that our simple computer built out of NAND gates could do two million things in the same time that only one thing could be done by a computer built out of nerves and synapses.

Another area where the difference between the mind and computers is quite obvious, is in the area of recognizing faces. The mind is very good at it. If you walk into a party with fifty people present, you will know in a matter of seconds whether you are among a group of friends or of strangers. A lot of research has been done into how people accomplish this feat, and a lot of very interesting information has been uncovered.

There is also a lot of speculation, and there are many fascinating theories about the underlying principles and mechanisms. But the complete and exact structures and functions have not been uncovered.

If you give a computer a picture file of a person, and then give it the same file again, it can compare the two files byte by byte and see that each byte in one file is exactly equal to the corresponding byte in the other file. But if you give the computer two pictures of the same person that were taken at different times, or from different angles, or with different lighting, or at different ages, then the bytes of the two files will not match up byte by byte. For the computer to determine that these two files represent the same person is a huge task. It has to run very complex programs that perform advanced mathematical functions on the files to find patterns in them, then figure out what those patterns might look like from different angles, then compare those things to every other face it has ever stored on its disk, pick the closest match, then determine if it's close enough to be the person or just someone that looks similar.

The point is that computers have a method of dealing with pictures based on the principles on which computers work. Using these principles alone has not yet yielded computers or software that can recognize a face with anywhere near the speed and accuracy of any ordinary person.

Voice recognition by computers is another technology that has come a long way, but has much further to go to rival what the mind does easily.

So in comparing a computer to a brain, it just doesn't look very likely that they operate on the same principles. The brain is very slow, there isn't any place to get the software to run it, and we don't see the types of problems we would expect with computer software errors.

In comparing a computer to the mind, the computer is vastly better at math, but the mind is better at dealing with faces and voices, and can contemplate the entirety of some entity that it has previously experienced.

Science fiction books and movies are full of machines that read minds or implant ideas into them, space ships with built-in talking computers and lifelike robots and androids. These machines have varying capabilities and some of the plots deal with the robot wrestling with consciousness, self-realization, emotions, etc. These machines seem to feel less than complete because they are just machines, and want desperately to become fully human. It's sort of a grown-up version of the children's classic "Pinocchio," the story about a marionette who wants to become a real boy.

But would it be possible to build such machines with a vastly expanded version of the technology that we used to build our simple computer?

Optimism is a great thing, and it should not be squashed, but a problem will not be susceptible to solution if you are using a methodology or technology that doesn't measure up to that problem. In the field of medicine, some diseases have been wiped out by antibiotics, others can be prevented by inoculations, but others still plague humanity despite the best of care and decades of research. And let's not even look into subjects like politics. Maybe more time is all that's needed, but you also have to look at the possibility that these problems either are unsolvable, or that the research has been looking in the wrong places for the answer.

As an example, many visions of the future have included people traveling around in flying cars. Actually, several types of flying cars have been built. But they are expensive, inefficient, noisy and very dangerous. They work on the same basic principles as helicopters. If two flying cars have any sort of a minor accident, everyone will die when both cars crash to the Earth. So today's aviation technology just won't result in a satisfactory flying car. Unless and until someone invents a cheap and reliable anti-gravity device, there will not be a mass market for flying cars and traffic on the roads will not be relieved.

If you want to build a machine that works just like a person, certainly the best way to do it would be to find out how the person works and then build a machine that works on the same principles, has parts that do the same things, and is wired up in the same way as a person.

When Thomas Edison invented the phonograph, he was dealing with the subject of sound. Sound is a vibration of the air. So he invented an apparatus that captured the vibrations in the air and transformed them into a vibrating groove on the surface of a wax cylinder. The sound could then be recreated by transferring the vibrations in the groove back into the air. The point is, that in order to recreate sound, he found out how sound worked, and then made a machine that worked on the same principle. Sound is a vibration, the groove in a phonograph is a vibration.

A lot of research has been done on the subject of what makes people tick. A lot of research has been done on the subject of how to make computers do the things that people do. A lot of things have been discovered and a lot of things have been invented. I do not want to minimize any of the work done, or results achieved in these areas.

But there are many things that have not yet been discovered or invented.

Many dead brains have been dissected and their parts have been studied and classified. The brain does contain nerve cells which move electricity from one place to another. This is a similarity between brains and computers. But research into the actual operation of living human brains is necessarily limited. Most observations have been made during surgeries that were necessitated by accident or disease. Many observations have been made of changes to behavior after an injury or disease has disabled certain parts of the brain. From this research, it has been possible to associate certain functions with certain areas of the brain.

But no one has discovered a bus, a clock, any registers, an ALU or RAM. The exact mechanism of memory in the brain remains a mystery. It has been shown that nerves grow new connections over time, and it is assumed that this is the mechanism of learning, but no one has been able to say that this particular nerve does this exact function, as we can do with the individual wires in a computer.

Everything that goes into a computer gets turned into one code or another. The keyboard generates one byte of ASCII per keystroke, a microphone generates 44,100 binary numbers per second, a color camera generates three binary numbers per pixel, 30 times a second, and so on. No one has isolated the use of any codes like ASCII, binary numbers, fonts or an instruction code in the brain. They may be there, but they have not been isolated. No one has traced a thought or located a memory in the same way that we could follow the operation of a program in a computer.

It is widely assumed that the brain works in some much more spread out way than a single computer, that there are thousands or billions of computer elements that cooperate and share the work. But such elements have not yet been located. In the world of computing, this idea is called 'parallel processing' and computers with dozens or hundreds of CPUs have been built. But these computers still haven't resulted in a human substitute.

Think of it all as a puzzle. How people work is one side of the puzzle. Making computers do things that people do is the other side of the puzzle. Pieces of the puzzle are being assembled on both sides. The problem is that as progress is being made on both sides, it looks more and more like these are two different puzzles, they are not coming together in the middle. They are not converging into a single picture.

The researchers are very aware of these developments. But when it comes to pop culture, people hear about new inventions all the time, and see the future portrayed in science fiction films, and the logical conclusion seems to be that research will continue to solve the problems one by one until in 10 or 20 or 30 years we will have our electro-mechanical friends. In the past century we conquered electricity, flight, space travel, chemistry, nuclear energy, etc. So why not the brain and/or mind? The research, however, is still at the stage where every time one new answer is found, it creates more than one more new question.

So it appears that whichever way we look at it, neither the brain nor the mind work on the same principles as computers as we know them. I say 'as we know them' because some other type of computer may be invented in the future. But all of the computers we have today come under the definition of 'Stored Program Digital Computers,' and all of the principles on which they operate have been presented in this book.

Still, none of this 'proves' that a synthetic human could never be built, it only means that the computer principles as presented in this book are not sufficient for the job. Some completely different type of device that operates on some completely different set of principles might be able to do it. But we can't comment on such a device until someone invents one.

Going back to a simpler question, do you remember Joe and the Thermos bottle? He thought that the Thermos had some kind of a temperature sensor, and a heater and cooler inside. But even if it had had all of that machinery in it, it still wouldn't "know" what to do, it would just be a mechanical device that turned on the heater or cooler depending on the temperature of the beverage placed in it.

A pair of scissors is a device that performs a function when made to do so. You put a finger and thumb in the holes and squeeze. The blades at the other end of the scissors move together and cut some paper or cloth or whatever it is that you have placed in their way. Do the scissors "know" how to cut shapes out of paper or how to make a dress out of cloth? Of course not, they just do what they're told.

Similarly, NAND gates don't "know" what they are doing, they just react to the electricity or lack of it placed on their inputs. If one gate doesn't know anything, then it doesn't matter how many of them you connect together, if one of them knows absolutely zero, a million of them will also know zero.

We use a lot of words that give human characteristics to our computers. We say that it "knows" things. We say it "remembers" things. We say that it "sees," and "understands." Even something as simple as a device adapter "listens" for its address to appear on the I/O bus, or a jump instruction "decides" what to do. There is nothing wrong with this as long as we know the truth of the matter.

Now that we know what is in a computer, and how it works, I think it is fairly obvious that the answer to the question "But How do it Know?" is simply "It doesn't know anything!"

Index

Made in the USA
Monee, IL
19 January 2023

25680028R00125